M. E. (Mary Elizabeth) Braddon

Joshua Haggard's daughter

Vol. III

M. E. (Mary Elizabeth) Braddon

Joshua Haggard's daughter
Vol. III

ISBN/EAN: 9783337050559

Printed in Europe, USA, Canada, Australia, Japan

Cover: Foto ©ninafisch / pixelio.de

More available books at **www.hansebooks.com**

JOSHUA HAGGARD'S DAUGHTER

A Novel

BY THE AUTHOR OF
'LADY AUDLEY'S SECRET'
ETC. ETC. ETC.

IN THREE VOLUMES
VOL. III.

LONDON
JOHN MAXWELL AND CO.
4 SHOE LANE, FLEET STREET
1876
[All rights reserved]

CONTENTS OF VOL. III.

CHAP.		PAGE
I.	Full of Scorpions	1
II.	'Farewell, Content'	21
III.	'We Two stood there with never a Third'	30
IV.	'It is a Basilisk unto mine Eye'	40
V.	'And yet I feel I fear'	56
VI.	The Wanderer's Return	76
VII.	'Where is thy Brother?'	90
VIII.	The Face in Oswald's Sketch-book	109
IX.	Repudiated	127
X.	What the Cowboy could tell	156
XI.	At his Door	175
XII.	An open Verdict	193
XIII.	Joshua stops his Watch	211
XIV.	Joshua's Confession	236
XV.	Carrying Peace and Pardon	254
XVI.	The Odour of Rosemary	261
XVII.	'Between two Worlds'	275
	Epilogue	295

JOSHUA HAGGARD'S DAUGHTER

CHAPTER I.

FULL OF SCORPIONS.

'WILL he come, will he come to see me?'

This was the question which Naomi asked herself when she arose next morning, to see another peerless summer day smiling at her, but to feel none of the joy of harvest; only a heart as dull and desolate as if she had awakened to find herself amidst some dwindled hope-forsaken band hemmed round by Arctic seas. What was summer to her, or harvest, or all the common joys of life—joys that gladden hearts which are *not* broken?

All through the feverish wakeful night the same doubt had agitated Naomi's mind. Might not her lover have repented and returned to her? So blessed a thing was just possible. He had loved her dearly once; surely that old love could not die. He had often told her that love was deathless. Fancy had gone astray, perhaps, and love had been true all the time. Absence had taught him that she was still dear. O, how tenderly she would have welcomed the returning prodigal, could she but be sure of his repentance, sure that her love could even yet make him happy! Thus argued hope; but despair took the other side. He had come back in secret for some evil purpose. He had come back to see Cynthia.

This day would show if he meant well or ill. If well, he would not fear to show himself at Mr. Haggard's house. He would come and make peace with his betrothed. O, long hours of waiting, between morning prayer and noontide—hours in which the simple household tasks were performed, while the girl's heart was given to alternate hope and despair! Would he come? Would he prove true and good, despite of all that had gone before!

Noon came, and dinner, and afternoon, and he

did not appear. Hope died in Naomi's breast. She went about the house listlessly, yet was too restless to sit long at her work. It happened to be a busy afternoon in the drapery department, and aunt Judith was too well employed behind the counter to observe her niece's idle moving to and fro, or else there would have been the small bitterness of that maiden lady's lectures superadded to the great bitterness of Naomi's despair.

Cynthia and Jim were in the garden. Those two were very friendly just now. The poor little stepmother clung to the honest outspoken lad in this time of cloud and brooding storm. Naomi's coldness cut her to the heart. She felt that there was a great gulf between her and her husband. Of Judith's dislike and distrust she was inwardly assured.

But Jim seemed fond of her, and he was of her husband's flesh and blood. The poor little timid soul went out to him in its loneliness.

'Do you really like me, James?' she asked today, as they were tying up the carnations in the long garden border, Cynthia's small face shaded by a dimity sun-bonnet.

'Liking isn't the word, Cynthia,' answered the boy. 'I'm uncommonly fond of you; and if you'd only show a little more spirit and make aunt Judith give up the housekeeping, I should have a still better opinion of you. Why should she stint us to one or two puddens a week, and those as hard as brickbats; and a fruit pasty once in a blue moon, when the garden's running over with gooseberries and may-dukes? It isn't her place to order the puddens. It's yours. It was all very well to be trodden under her foot when we were orphans; but you're our mother now, and you ought to stand by us. Why don't we have bacon and fried potatoes for breakfast, like Christians? She'd let a whole side go rusty before she'd give us the benefit of it. And my father sits at the table and starves himself, and quotes William Law to show that starvation is a Christian duty. I've no patience! I'm sure I wonder I've grown up the fine young man I am upon such short commons.'

Jim came into the house half an hour later, and found Naomi in the parlour. She was standing by the window idle, her work in her hands, staring absently at the bend in the road yonder, by which Oswald used to come on Herne the Hunter. Poor old faithful Herne! the tears came into her eyes when she thought of him. He had been turned out to grass, and she had seen him looking over gaps in the hedge, a haggard unkempt beast. She had called him and coaxed him, and held out her hand to invite his approach; and he had come with a shy sidelong gait close up to her, and even sniffed at her in a friendly way, and then shot off like a sky-rocket before she could caress his honest gray nose.

Jim burst into the parlour like a whirlwind.

'I thought you was fond of those crinkly harts-tongues I got for you?' he exclaimed, breathless with indignation.

'So I am, Jim; very fond of them.'

'Then you'd better get a bit of black stuff out of the shop and make yourself a mourning-gown!'

'Are they dead?'

'They're as near it as anything in the fern line can be—as yellow as the inside of a poached egg, and half eaten by snails. How long is it since you've been in the wilderness?'

'I don't know: a few days—a week, perhaps.'

'You're a nice young woman for an industrious brother to toil for! The place is as dry as an ash-pit. What's the use of my getting you fine specimens, if this is the way you treat 'em? There's the parsley-fern crinkled up like a bit of whity-brown paper. Cynthia and I have been giving the things a good dowsing; but they've been shamefully neglected. I should have thought you could have found time to look after them. You're not in the business,' concluded Jim, with a superior air.

'Don't be cross, Jim,' faltered Naomi gently. 'It was wrong of me to neglect the ferns that you've taken such trouble to set for me; but I have not done any gardening lately; I have not been feeling well enough—'

And here Naomi burst into tears—Naomi, with whom tears were so rare.

Jim had his arms round her in a moment, and was hugging her like an affectionate bruin.

'There, there, there!' he cried; 'don't fret. I oughtn't to have been so cross. You've had your troubles lately—father going and breaking off your marriage without rhyme or reason. Nobody ever heard of such tyranny. I'll be sworn William Law, the father of Methodism, is at the bottom of it. Suffering is good for us. It's blessed to deny ourselves. And my poor little sister mustn't marry the man she loves! Cheer up, Naomi; it will all come right in the end, I daresay, though things are going crooked now. Don't worry about the wilderness. Cynthia and I are making things tidy—weeding and watering, and training the creepers over the rockwork. You can come down and look at us, if you like; it will cheer you up a bit.'

'I'll come presently, Jim dear,' answered Naomi, drying her tears.

'Be sure you do,' said Jim; and then he hurried back to his work.

Naomi sat in the parlour for a quarter of an hour or so. She shed no more tears, but sat with dry eyes looking straight before her.

Why had he come back? Not for her—O, not for her!

The day was nearly done. She could hear the rattling of teacups in the pantry. Sally was getting her tray ready. That meant half-past four o'clock. Naomi rose with a long heavy sigh, and went out into the garden. It was to please her brother she went. There was no pleasure or interest for her in earth or sky.

She walked slowly down the long straight garden path, where the clove carnations and double stocks were in their glory, and through the little orchard to the wilderness. Jim was hard at work—the perspiration running down his forehead, his coat off, and his shirt-sleeves rolled up to the elbow—dividing great tufts of primroses and overgrown hartstongue. Cynthia was on her knees weeding, a pretty picture of youth and fairness in the yellow sunlight.

Naomi stood and looked at her. What was the charm in her that had lured her false lover? Could the eye of another woman see the bait that had won weak and fickle man; the enchantment which had wrought alike upon the strong man in his meridian of knowledge and wisdom and the youth in his folly?

Yes, the charm revealed itself even to the cold eye of a resentful rival. It was not so much absolute beauty which allured in this nameless waif as a soft and gracious innocence, a flower-like loveliness, that stole upon mind and heart unawares.

She charmed the senses, as roses and lilies do in the early morning while the dew is still on them. She appealed to the eye and held it, like some picture which, in a long gallery, stands out from all other images, and transfixes the spectator. She stole upon the soul like music heard afar off on a river, in the still summer night.

Nor was it this outward charm of perfect fairness and grace only which attracted. The soft lovableness of her disposition accorded with the tender grace of her beauty. She had the clinging affectionateness of a soft and yielding nature; a humility of spirit which made her ready to reverence the strong; a tenderness of heart which inclined her to pity the weak. In one word she was lovable—a woman created to be loved.

Naomi stood and looked at her, full of bitter thoughts. For the first time in her life she envied the gifts of another. She felt all the good things that Providence had given her of no account when weighed against the bewitchment of fair looks and winning ways.

'How wicked I am growing!' she thought, shocked at her own bitterness.

'There!' exclaimed Jim, pulling down his shirt-sleeves; 'I think I have done a tidy afternoon's work. You'll have oceans of primroses next year, sis.'

'If they don't all die,' said Naomi, not hopefully. 'Do you think it's quite the right time for moving them?'

'Primroses!' cried Jim. 'As if you could hurt a primrose! I know what I am about, sister. They wouldn't take any harm by my moving if they were the delicatest flowers in a hot-house.'

He pulled on his coat, put away trowel and rake, and came out of the wild garden into the orchard. Cynthia rose too, with an absent-minded sigh, and followed him.

'Now look here, little stepmother,' he said, in his patronising way; 'you'd better go in and make yourself tidy for tea, while I show Naomi what I have done to her primroses.'

Cynthia obeyed without a word, and left them.

Jim tucked his sister's arm under his own, and began to perambulate the orchard.

'What's the matter, Jim?'

'Cheer up, old woman; I've got some good news for you. I won't see you trampled upon, not if I can help it. I won't have your early affections blighted, and young Pentreath sent to the right-about, if I can prevent it. Don't be afraid, sis; I'll stand by you.'

'Jim, what do you mean?' cried Naomi piteously.

'I've got a letter for you.'

Naomi's heart leapt with sudden overwhelming joy. Oswald had written. Thank God, thank God! She was not utterly forgotten.

'A letter, Jim?' clasping his arm rapturously. 'How did it come?'

'How should it come? He brought it himself, of course.'

'And gave it to you? You saw him? Dear, dear Jim, tell me all about it. How is he looking, ill or well?'

'White and fagged; as if he'd been going to the

—well, you know—all the time he's been in London. I only just caught a glimpse of him above the wall.'

'And he gave you the letter—'

'No, that's the fun of it. He didn't see me. It was just as I came back to the wilderness after I left you in the parlour. Cynthia was sitting reading on the bench yonder. Just as I came to the gate, I saw a pale face look over the wall; and then a white hand went up and threw something over. It fell among the ferns, not a yard from stepmother. But she never saw it; that was the lark. Her nose was in her book, poetry or some such trash. I gave a whistle, and off went my gentleman like a shot—scared away.'

'And what became of the letter?'

'Why, I picked it up unbeknown to Cynthia, when her back was turned. It's wrapped round a stone. There's no address on it—too artful for that —but I knew the party it was meant for.'

'Are you sure it's for me?' asked Naomi, trembling a little. That exceeding great joy fainted in her heart. A letter unaddressed, and thrown at Cynthia's feet!

'Of course it's for you. Stepmother sat with her back to the wall, and her head and shoulders smothered in that great sun-bonnet of hers. He might easy take her for you.'

'Give me the letter, dear,' said Naomi, with suppressed eagerness.

He handed her a little parcel—a goodish-sized pebble packed neatly in a sheet of letter-paper, and carefully sealed with the well-known coat-of-arms which had hung a year ago from the Squire's fob.

'Ain't you going to read it?' demanded Jim, as his sister stood looking at the packet.

'Not just yet, dear. I had rather read it when I am quite alone.'

'O my!' ejaculated Jim. 'For fear some of the love should run over, like clouted cream that hasn't set properly. What it is to be in love! Well, sis, I'll leave you to the enjoyment of your love-letter, while I go and clean myself.'

He ran off, leaving Naomi alone in the orchard. Fear held her hand for a moment, though hope whispered that this little packet was full of comfort and sweetness. It had fallen at Cynthia's feet, said fear. Was it not possible that it had been meant for Cynthia?

She broke the seal and carefully unfolded the sheet of Bath post—the fair wide paper which our forefathers used when letters were worth having.

It was a letter of three pages, written by a hand which betrayed its owner's emotion. Naomi's eyes shone with an angry light as they hurried over the lines. There was a name written here and there—a hateful name, that told her the letter was not for her —'My Cynthia;' 'My Cynthia—mine by that mutual love which is our mutual sorrow!'

'Villain and traitor!' cried Naomi, with a burst of passion which transformed her.

Had he stood before her in that moment, and she armed, she could have stabbed him. This Naomi, who could have laid down her life to accomplish some good and great thing, was, for this one instant, capable of murder.

Such cruel perfidy, such heartless treachery, such shameless iniquity, outraged her sense of justice. It seemed to her as if Heaven had created a monster.

She had not yet read the letter, but Cynthia's name stood out from the tremulous lines as if it had been written in fire. Slowly, with her hand pressed against her burning forehead, in the effort to keep brain and understanding clear, she addressed herself to the hateful task.

She would know the lowest deep of man's infamy: a lover who could forsake his sworn love; a man, calling himself a gentleman, who could try to seduce a good man's wife.

The letter was incoherent, passionate—despair's foolish appeal against Fate:

'I must see you once again—yes, dearest, at whatever hazard to you or me, at whatever cost. I have made up my mind to live and die far away from the dear place that holds you. The wide, bleak, barren sea shall roll between me and my beloved. I am going to America; that is far enough, surely! Death could part us no wider than the Atlantic. I shall look at that great sea, and think how the green waves roll up the golden sands of home and kiss your feet; how the white spray blows into your hair and caresses you like a cloud—and I am no Jove, to be in that cloud, love. I shall be severed from you for ever. But before I sail for the other side of the sea I must see you once more; yes, Cynthia, my Cynthia —mine by that mutual love which is our mutual sorrow—I must see you once more, clasp your hand and say farewell; bless you, and be blessed by you. Trust me, trust me, my beloved, with but one meeting. There shall no evil word be spoken; you shall not even hear me complain against Fate. I will only take your hand in mine and say good-bye. Vain blessing, you will say; but, dearest love, the memory of that moment will comfort me in weary days and nights to come. I would but know that you pity and forgive and pray for me; and that, if Fate had willed it so, you might have loved me. It will be like a parting between two friends when one is doomed to die. I shall think the executioner is waiting at the door, and the death-bell ready to toll. O dear love, by thy tender and pitying heart, I adjure thee, grant me this last prayer! Thy Werther, despairing unto death, pleads to thee!

'I have come back to Devonshire for this only—

to see you once more. I have taken my passage for New York. All is settled; nothing can alter my decision. I am not weak enough, or guilty enough, to remain within reach of you. I thought that in London I might forget; but your image followed me everywhere I went; in crowds or in solitudes, you were always near; nothing but a lifelong exile can cure my wound or expiate my guilt.

'Let me see you, beloved one. I shall contrive to convey this letter to you by some means in the course of to-day. Meet me to-morrow afternoon; and to-morrow night, by the coach which starts from the First and Last at eight o'clock, I will leave Combhaven for ever. Your afternoons are always free; I shall wait for you, from two to four o'clock, on the common beyond Matcherly Wood, near the old shaft. It is rather far for you to come, but I think it is the safest place for our meeting. No one ever comes there but a stray cow-boy in quest of his cattle.

'Come, dearest; it is the only boon you can bestow upon one whose heart you have broken unawares.—Yours till death,   OSWALD.'

This was the letter. Naomi read it slowly to the end, and then put it in her pocket.

A shrill shriek from the house-door roused her from abstraction.

'Naomi, are you coming?' at the top of aunt Judith's high-pitched voice.

'We never do have our teas like Christians nowadays!' complained Miss Haggard, as Naomi came into the parlour breathless. 'Have you seen another ghost, girl?' she asked, staring at her niece. 'You look as white as a yard of calico. Here's your father not home to his tea again; that makes the third time this week.'

'He is attending to his duty, no doubt, aunt.'

'Who says he isn't? But I wish he could contrive to combine duty with punctuality at meals. I hate a disorderly table.'

Joshua came in just as they had finished their meal. His large cup of tea had been put on one side for him, covered with a saucer. He sat down in his armchair and drank his tea in silence. He was looking exhausted and weary.

'I am afraid you have had a hard afternoon's

work, Joshua,' Cynthia said, sitting down beside him timidly.

'I have been in the house of death, my dear; that is always trying to weak humanity. And I have walked a long way in the sun.'

Naomi sat by the window darning Jim's stockings. Aunt Judith retired to the drapery department. Joshua leant back in his chair, with closed eyes. Cynthia took up a book; it was Milton's *Paradise Lost,* one of the few imaginative works of which Mr. Haggard did not disapprove.

They sat thus for some time, in a silence only broken by the lowing of distant cattle and the gentle lapping of summer waves upon the pebbly beach. Then Jim looked in at the door and called Cynthia. She rose quickly and went out to him, and Naomi was alone with her father.

This was the opportunity she had been waiting for. After reading Oswald's letter she had come to a desperate resolve. These lofty natures have a touch of hardness in their composition sometimes. A sense of immunity from sin and weakness makes them stony-hearted judges of erring humanity. Oswald's wrongdoing had awakened that latent element of hardness in Naomi's nature. She thought she was only doing her duty in taking desperate measures. Or was it jealousy which put on a mask and called itself justice? She took the letter out of her pocket, and looked at her father. He was not asleep, only resting with closed eyes.

'Father,' said Naomi, in a low voice, 'here is a letter which has come to me by accident, and which I think you ought to see. It is from Oswald to your wife.'

She put the letter into his hand and left him. She dared not await the issue of her act.

CHAPTER II.

'FAREWELL, CONTENT.'

Joshua read the letter slowly, every word going to his heart like the thrust of a knife. He had been told that a man had addressed a confession of guilty love to his wife, and the knowledge that this thing had been had preyed upon him like a corroding poison. But even in all he had suffered since Judith's revelation he had never realised the greatness of the wrong as he did now, with the betrayer's letter in his hand, the audacious confession deliberately set down in black and white.

'He dared to write this!' he muttered. 'He dared—to my wife! O God! how low she must have fallen in his esteem before he wrote this letter!'

Here was the cruellest sting. Could Oswald have penned this passionate appeal had he not been sure of a hearing? Did not this letter imply that he knew himself beloved? Ay, there were the abhorrent words burning the paper: 'That mutual love, which is our mutual sorrow!' This villain made very sure that he was loved. Must he not have been so assured before he dared to ask an honest woman to grant him a secret meeting?

Joshua Haggard sat with the letter in his hand, and a look in those dark eyes of his—a lurid fire under black lowering brows—which would have struck terror to the hearts of his admiring flock could they have seen their shepherd in his lonely agony. What was he to do—how find revenge great enough for this gigantic wrong? Revenge was not the thought in his mind; retribution, justice rather, was what he demanded. He felt himself like Orestes, privileged, nay appointed, to slay. The furies might come afterwards, but in this present hour it seemed to him that he might claim this man's blood.

That gentlemanlike institution, the duel, was in full force in Joshua's day. It was but a year or so since a couple of English dukes had tried to murder each other in a pit in Hyde Park. Had he been a man of the world, nothing would have been clearer or more easy than his course. But for the shepherd of souls, the preacher of peace, to take up the sword! Would it not be the renunciation of those principles for which he had lived? How often from his pulpit had he anathematised the slayer of his brother, hurled his thunders against that corrupt society in which murder could be deemed honourable!

He sat with the letter in his hand, and all was dark before him. Could he ever trust his wife again?—believe in her purity, cherish with a fond and almost fatherly pride that sweet and girlish innocence, that utter ignorance of evil, the freshness and beauty of life's morning, which had first won his love? Never more—never more! His Eve had gathered the fatal fruit; the serpent had lifted his venomous crest from among the flowers; the glory of life's paradise had faded. Never more could he love, or worship, or trust. Henceforth he must hold her loathly. If this letter had reached her, how would she have received it? Would she have listened to the tempter's pleading? Would she have stolen in secret to meet him, to hear his poisonous vows, to pity his weak unmanly lamentings?

'I should like to know that,' he said to himself; 'I should like to know how she would have answered this letter.'

And then it occurred to him that he might easily put her to the test. The seal had been broken, but the paper round it was untorn. It would be easy to reseal the letter, making the second seal just a little larger than the first; and Cynthia would not examine the outside of the letter too closely.

He lighted a candle and resealed the violated letter; then paused for a moment or so, wondering how he should get it conveyed to his wife. 'She shall find it somewhere,' he thought. 'Her guilty conscience will tell her it is from her lover. He may have written to her before, perhaps. God only knows the greatness of her sin—God who made us, and knows the blackness of our unregenerate hearts. And I thought that there could be one exempt—one free from humanity's universal taint. Fool, fool, fool!'

He went slowly up-stairs to the bedchamber, the airy orderly room, with its substantial old-fashioned furniture and look of homely comfort—the room that had once been his father's. There hung the old grocer's turnip-shaped silver watch on the mahogany stand upon the mantelpiece, ticking with as lusty a beat as when its sturdy proprietor carried it in his ample drab-cloth fob. There were the samplers which testified to the industry and skill of Joshua's mother and Joshua's wife—the pyramidal apple-trees innocent of leaves, the angular figures of Adam and Eve in the garden, with a curly serpent standing on tip-tail between them. The evening sun shone into the room, and glorified the gaudy sunflowers on the chintz bed-furniture, and glittered on the brazen handles of Joshua's escritoire. A bowl of freshly-gathered roses and carnations on the table perfumed all the room. Joshua knew whose busy hand had plucked the flowers, and the sight of them smote him with an aching pain. O, wounded heart, for which every new thought was a new torture!

The escritoire stood open, and there was the *Sorrows of Werther*, lying where he had placed it after his long night of waking. There had been no need for Cynthia to hide the book any more. It had told its story.

Joshua's sombre glance lighted on the volume. 'Accursed book that taught them to sin!' he exclaimed; 'they might never have fathomed the wickedness of their own hearts but for thee.'

This was hard upon the innocent and noble Charlotte, the misguided but generous Werther.

A thought full of bitterness and anger came into Joshua's mind as he looked at *Werther*. He would put Oswald's letter between the leaves of that detested book. She would find it there, he felt assured; the book was her own love-story, it talked to her of her lover. He could fancy her hanging over the pages, sucking poisonous sweetness from every line. Werther and Oswald were, in Joshua's mind, one.

He put the letter in the book, and was going slowly down-stairs, when he stopped, with his hand upon the banisters, and pondered for a minute or so.

The thought came over him that he could not pray with his household, or teach or exhort them to-night. It was as if an evil spirit were at his shoulder forbidding him that holy and familiar exercise. He felt that it would have been a kind of profanation to lay his hand upon the Bible, that anchor of his life, which had never before seemed insufficient mooring for his wind-driven bark.

'Not to-night,' he muttered to himself—'not to-night.'

He called over the stairs to his daughter, who had just come in from the garden.

'Tell your aunt to read a chapter and a psalm, Naomi,' he said; 'I am too ill to come down-stairs again to-night.'

Naomi hurried to him, full of apprehension.

'Dearest father, what is the matter? Can I do anything? can I get you anything?'

Conscience smote her. Why had she afflicted him by the sight of that wicked letter? It would have been better to have taken it to Cynthia, and spoken words of Christian reproof and warning. Why had she made him, her dearest upon earth, to suffer?

'No, my dear, you can do nothing. It is the mind that is ill at ease, not the body. My soul is too dark to hold communion with her God. The blow has been heavy.'

'Dear father, it was so wicked of me to show you the letter—an evil revengeful act. And, after all, the sin may not be so deep as it seems to us. They are but children—weak, foolish, easily led astray. Let us pity and forgive them.'

'I may come—some day, when I am old and doting—to pity her. I can never forgive him.'

He put his daughter aside, went into his bedroom, and shut the door. Naomi dared not follow him. She went slowly down-stairs, greatly troubled.

It is one thing to launch the thunderbolt, and another to survey the ruin the bolt has made.

Joshua Haggard turned his face to the wall, and gave himself up to darkest thoughts. He rose soon after daybreak, and his first look was directed to *Werther*. The letter was gone. Yes; there was nothing now between the pages but a few faded rose-leaves and withered fern tendrils, which marked a favourite passage here and there.

He looked from the book to his wife, lying with her face turned from the light, and one round white arm, dimpled like a young child's, thrown above her head. Was she sleeping placidly with that guilty secret in her breast, or only pretending to sleep? He could not tell.

'She is all dissimulation,' he thought, 'fairest seeming, sweetest show—bitter as ashes within!'

CHAPTER III.

'WE TWO STOOD THERE WITH NEVER A THIRD.'

IN the sultry August afternoon—earth glorious in the full power of the sunshine—Oswald Pentreath went up to Matcherly Common. It was a long walk and a hot one, but in this land of beauty there were many welcome spots of shade—cool lanes shadowed by tangled greenery, natural arcades of oak and hawthorn, wild apple and elderberry, from which he could look out on the glittering sea, almost intolerable in its sunlit splendour. There was the wood to cross; a deep and cool retreat, where interwoven boughs made summer days seem a perpetual evensong. Only here and there stole a shaft of vivid light through the beechen branches; while now and then the ruddy fur of a squirrel shot like a flash of colour through the gloom.

Oswald walked slowly, his hands clasped behind

his back, giving himself up to the soft influence of the scene and hour, and thinking of Cynthia.

Would she grant his prayer? Would she meet him? Love and hope said yes; and the thought of the meeting was rapture, though despair lay beyond it. He was to die to-night—or at least all of him that made life worth having—but he was to be happy first; happy for the brief span of time in which he could hold her in his arms and press one kiss upon her innocent brow, and bless her and leave her.

The thought that his letter might reach the wrong hands had not occurred to him. He had seen Cynthia sitting in the wilderness, and had thrown his letter almost at her feet; Jim's approach had made him retreat suddenly, but it had never struck him that Cynthia might not see the letter, and that Jim might.

The common was on high ground rising above the wood—a broad tract of undulating land clothed with furze, and with a pool of water here and there, just like that stretch of heath, far away, where Joshua Haggard had found his second wife. The mines, whose deserted shafts disfigured this billowy expanse of golden bloom, had not been worked since Watt first applied steam to mining. They had yielded well enough in their day, had made some men rich and ruined others; and there stood the dilapidated engine-houses with their tall chimneys, wide apart across the common, like sentinel towers on the coast of a golden sea.

Cynthia was there. Oswald found her sitting on a yellow bank at the base of the abandoned shaft, sitting with a book open in her lap, trying to read. She started up, as he came towards her, with a frightened look, as if his coming had been a surprise to her, and stood before him very pale, with clasped hands.

' Dearest, best, how shall I thank you !' he cried, taking her hands and kissing them in a rapture of gratitude.

' Do not thank me at all, Oswald; indeed, I am afraid I have done very wrong in coming; you ought not to have asked me, you ought never to have come back to Combhaven, unless it was in your heart to be true to Naomi. O Oswald, why can you not love her as she deserves to be loved, as you did once love her? She is so good, so noble, like my dear husband in all high thoughts. Why cannot your heart come back to her? Why should we all be miserable because you are inconstant?'

The poor little soul had come here to say this. She had come with a clear and honest purpose in her mind—come to bring the wanderer back to the path of duty.

'Can a man help his fate?' said Oswald gloomily. 'It is my fate to love you. I shall love you till I die. But don't be frightened, Cynthia; I will be the cause of misery to none of you. I am going to America; my mind is quite made up on that point.'

'And you will break Naomi's heart. If you could see the change in her since you left us you could not help being sorry.'

'I am sorry. My soul is sick with sorrow. But my heart cannot go back to Naomi. It never was hers. I never knew what love meant till I loved you. I made the fatal error of mistaking affection for love. I am sorry for her; sorry that I have wronged so noble a creature; sorry for the loss of that peaceful life which I once thought to share with her. But I cannot go back. You might as well ask me to be a child again. The star of my manhood shone upon me when I saw you.'

'I wish I were wiser,' said Cynthia sadly; 'I wish I could speak as I feel I ought to speak; I might convince you then, perhaps.'

'Not if you had the eloquence of Brougham and the wisdom of Bacon. Naomi and I are parted for ever, dearest, and at her own desire. It is best that it should be so. Providence has been good to me in loosening a bond that would have made two lives miserable.'

And then he said no more about Naomi, but began to talk of himself, and love, and fate, and parting, and despair. Foolish words that have been said so often, empty breath for the most part, bearing no result upon this earth save idle sorrow and wasted tears, yet which mean so much for the speaker and the one who listens. Cynthia had come there to hear no such passionate complaints and protestations. She had come intent upon delivering her pious lecture, talking to him of grace and redemption, and the sacred stream which washes away all sin, and winning him back to duty and Naomi. Yet she lingered and heard him. It was the last time. They were parting for ever. Who should blame them for this one half-hour, which would stand hereafter like a chasm in the life of each, dividing youth and passion from sober age and duty? It could matter to no one that they had met thus, and thus parted.

'You will try to lead a good life?' pleaded Cynthia, when Oswald had told his pitiful story—told how he had honestly striven to forget her, and had failed; 'you will cling to the cross? O, let me think when you are far away, across that wide cruel sea, that your soul is safe, that you are one of the elect, that I shall meet you where the seas are jasper, and the glory of the Lamb lights the shining streets! You will try to be good, Oswald? Promise me that!'

'I would wear raiment of camel's-hair and a hempen girdle for your sake, dearest.'

'You will go to chapel—church is so cold and dull; it has no awakening power, it does not call the lost home? You will seek out some stirring preacher like Joshua, and let him lead you to the sheltering rock, and you will drink the living water and be saved?'

Oswald looked down at the fair young face lifted to his with such utter earnestness, not one thought of earth in the pleading soul; only thorough and implicit belief in something higher and better than earth, a prize to be struggled for and won. In that Greek race in which the runners carried lighted lamps in their hands, they were the winners who reached the goal with their lamps still burning. So in the Christian race, the light once quenched there is but little hope for the runner. It might be safely said of Cynthia, as she looked up at her lover with innocent eyes, charging him to be thoughtful for eternity, that her lamp still burned with purest light.

Oswald looked down at her through a mist of tears.

'Yes,' he said, 'for your sake I will try to make myself fit for heaven. I have been careless of these things. I meant to let Naomi make me a Christian, but she was to have had all the trouble. But for your sake, to meet you hereafter in a fairer world, to see this dear face again shining amidst the angel-faces, I will struggle, I will strive to make my life worthier and better.'

'God bless and comfort you, and establish you in well-doing!' said Cynthia. 'And now good-bye. I must not stay a moment longer; I have been too long already.'

She looked at her watch. Four o'clock, and she had three miles to walk before five. There would be much astonishment and questioning if she was not punctual in her appearance at the tea-table.

'You will let me walk through the wood with you?'

'No; what would be the use? I have said all I had to say. It would only make us more unhappy.'

'It would give us one more hour together,' said Oswald; 'an hour in paradise.'

'The Christian's paradise is to be reached by thornier paths than those through Matcherly Wood,' answered Cynthia, with a reproving air. 'Good-bye, Oswald.'

Her earnestness dominated him, weak and childish as she looked, with the fair hair clustering in baby curls under the shady cottage-bonnet. Very soft and gentle, but very firm at the same time, she seemed, in her simple straightforwardness of purpose; and Oswald obeyed her.

'Since it must be so, then, good-bye,' he said gloomily. 'I promised that I would be content with a brief farewell, such as condemned criminals have. You have given me a little sermon into the bargain. I ought to be more than satisfied. Farewell, my best beloved; the seas will roll between us soon, and there will be nothing left for me but the picture and memory of to-day; nothing but the dreams that haunt my pillow—the sweet unreal presence of her I love.'

He took her to his breast, she having no more force to resist those circling arms than a lily to recoil from the hand that gathers it; took her gently and solemnly to his heart, and pressed his lips on her forehead. It was a long and fervent kiss; but if there was passion in it, that passion was no base or sensual feeling; only the passion of a great love and a deep despair.

'Bless you, my darling!' he cried. 'God bless you and guard you, and make all days and paths pleasant and peaceful for you when I am far away!'

And so they parted—for ever. Unhappily, there was one who saw the lingering meeting, the fond embrace, the fervent kiss, but could not hear the words that went with them.

CHAPTER IV.

'IT IS A BASILISK UNTO MINE EYE.'

TRANQUIL and monotonous days hung like a cloud upon the little household of Combhaven. The daily round of labour, of eating and drinking in a spare and Spartan fashion, of praying and preaching, went on with pitiless regularity; but of household joys there were none, of family love but little. A gloomy change had come over Joshua Haggard. He was still the enthusiastic apostle of Primitive Methodism; a man ready to go out and preach the Gospel in wild and barbarous places, to be the bearer of glad tidings to those who despised and rejected such messengers, to be hooted by a brutal rabble, if need were, and driven from village to village at peril of his life, and to escape from his persecutors by the skin of his teeth, as John Wesley did, more than once, in his long and difficult career. He was ready to endure all things. Day by day his discourses grew more fervid, but, alas, more darkly fraught with a message which was not glad tidings—the message of an offended and an avenging God. Christ, the Saviour, was almost excluded from the preacher's exhortations. When he talked of man's Redeemer it was as of one who turned His face from a sinful world, in which there were very few to be saved. If he had lived in that awful time before the Deluge, when all the earth was peopled with reprobates, he could hardly have been more despairing of humanity's ultimate destiny.

His flock were in nowise offended by this gloomy view of their spiritual condition, although it implied so mean an opinion of their personal merits and conduct. The more vehemently threatening Joshua Haggard's sermons became, the more eagerly the sinners crowded to hear him. It was as if they liked to hear themselves upbraided and denounced. Perhaps everybody saw the barbed shaft fly straight to the gold of a neighbour's heart, and did not feel it rankling in his own. When Joshua talked of the frivolity and extravagance of an unregenerate race, Mrs. Pycroft thought of Mrs. Spradgers's last new bonnet, which was clearly a superfluous and culpable outlay; such bonnet not being due to Mrs. Spradgers, from an economic point of view, until Advent Sunday, whereas the lady had flaunted it before the disapproving eyes of the flock early in October. If Joshua denounced sensuality and the vile indulgence of earthly desires, Mrs. Pentelow's thoughts flew at once to the Polwhele family, who were known to have hot suppers—squab-pies and other savoury meats—every night in the week. You could see the grease oozing out of their complexions on warm Sunday afternoons, as if digestion as well as respiration were a function of the skin.

From the day when he gave up humanity for lost, and plainly told them so, Joshua's popularity increased in a marked degree. The darker his doctrines grew, the better his congregation liked to hear him. It was not milk for babes which they wanted, but strong meat for men of iron thews and sinews, and women with vigorous constitutions and masculine strength of mind. They liked to hear that the devil was among them, at their shoulders, prompting them to evil, fighting for the mastery of their souls.

'I can see him, I can feel his presence,' cried

Joshua, in a passion of despairing ecstasy. 'He is among us; his sulphurous breath burns me with a foretaste of eternal fire; his whisper hisses in my ear as the serpent's hiss stole into the ear of Eve. He will not loose his hold. He is fighting for the possession of my soul; he is striving to drag me down into the pit. What shall I do to be saved? How shall I win the fight against so omnipotent an adversary—omnipotent to destroy, omnipotent to enthral and enchain souls? He wants to people hell, my brethren. He is not content with his victory over willing sinners; the profligates and harlots are too pitiful a prey for him! He wants to have the virtuous man in his net. He would have liked to get John Wesley, or George Whitfield, or William Law. He tried for them, as he is trying for us. He is a fallen angel himself, and it pleases him to entrap men of high estate—to take the Christian in his toils—to make the white scarlet, and the wool like unto blood.'

Naomi heard and shuddered. Was this her father, who had once preached infinite faith in God's mercy, in Christ's redeeming grace? He talked now as if mankind were abandoned as a prey to the Evil One, with no guardian and champion to protect and save, no all-merciful Judge to adjust the balance; as if humanity, forgotten by God, were left to struggle single-handed against the devices of the great Enemy. Of our ever-interceding Redeemer, of guardian angels and ministering spirits, and saints who had fought and conquered, Joshua now rarely spoke. He described a world given over to the Prince of Darkness.

Nor was this the only change which Naomi beheld with remorseful grief, believing herself in somewise to blame for this gloomy transformation. In his home as well as in his pulpit the minister was a new man. It was not in his nature to become a domestic tyrant. He interfered with no one's liberty or comfort; but he sat in his domestic circle like a statue, he banished all cheerfulness by his silent presence, he breathed an atmosphere of gloom.

Even Judith regretted this alteration in her brother's temper, though she had been apt in happier days to think him far too easy and indulgent a father. She, like Naomi, had her moments of remorse, thinking the change her work. Better perhaps if she had held her tongue about that foolish young man, and let time and Providence cure him of his folly. Naomi's marriage would have been a feather in the family cap; and although Miss Haggard had been disposed to begrudge her niece this exaltation, it was a trial to receive the condolences of friends whose affected sympathy thinly disguised their inward satisfaction. Yes, taking all things into consideration, Judith was sorry she had not held her peace. She had acted for the best, of course—when had she ever done otherwise?—but the worst had come of it instead of the best.

Cynthia bore her cross and made no murmur, and had neither kindness nor pity for any one except James Haggard, who thought it a hard thing that his pretty young stepmother should lead so dreary a life. She had not even the business and the delightful consciousness of increasing profits to console her, nor the power to restore exhausted nature with a surreptitious handful of figs or pudding-raisins when the dinner had been more than usually Spartan. James was sorry for the 'poor little woman,' as he called her, and was kind to her always, for which grace she rewarded him with heartfelt affection.

But her husband — the teacher, master, and friend, whom she had loved so dearly, reverenced so deeply, and to whom, even when weak enough to pity and return Oswald's romantic passion, she had always rendered homage and affection—had withdrawn his favour from her; he loved her no longer; he was doubtless sorry that he had linked himself to so weak and useless a creature.

'What am I in his life?' she asked herself, in deepest despondency. 'I cannot even keep his house for him; others do that. I sit by his fireside a useless intruder. He will not let me share in his higher life; if I ask him about the books he reads, or talk to him about our religion, I can see a disdainful sneer upon his lip. Sometimes I think that he is getting to hate me.'

This thought was poison. Cynthia searched her life to see in what article of it she had offended her husband, and could discover no cause for his anger. That she had erred in letting Oswald love her, in letting her heart go out to him, she knew, and had repented of her sin with many tears; and, having bidden the sinner an eternal farewell, deemed that error a thing of the past, repented of, and in somewise atoned. She did not believe that jealousy was the cause of her husband's estrangement. Jealousy was allied to love, and her great fear was that Joshua hated her. She did not know that there is a kind of jealousy, and that which has its root in the deepest love, which puts on the garb of hate, and has not seldom culminated in murder—such jealousy as made Othello strike Desdemona before the Venetian emissaries, the passion of strong natures.

She endured her husband's unkindness with a sweet submission which might have softened a sterner temper than Joshua's, and would assuredly have melted him but for the corroding influence of a sleepless jealousy—jealousy of the past, jealousy of a ghost—for the departed Oswald was nothing more than a shade.

Joshua had said no word to his daughter about Oswald's letter. All through that day on which Cynthia went to Matcherly Common, Naomi had been full of anxiety and fear. How would her father act? Would his anger against Oswald take any violent shape? That was assuredly a contingency to be dreaded, an evil she had not foreseen when she gave Joshua the letter. But passion is fatally blind. The harm being done, she could see the possible danger plainly enough.

All through the long summer day she was restless and watchful, fearing she knew not what, or rather not daring to tell herself what she feared. The morning went by very quietly: Cynthia sitting in the parlour, sewing; Naomi busy about her usual household labours. She went in and out of the parlour a good many times, and always found Cynthia in the same attitude, working assiduously.

Had Joshua spoken to his wife about the letter?

Yes; Naomi thought he had. There was one bright spot of colour on Cynthia's pale cheek that told of agitation studiously suppressed. Once when Naomi spoke to her she answered absently. She must know something about the letter, Naomi thought.

After dinner Cynthia went up to her bedroom, and came down in five minutes with her bonnet on.

It was a busy afternoon in the shop. Aunt Judith and Jim had returned to their duties, and Joshua had gone out. There was only Naomi in the parlour when Cynthia came down ready for her walk.

'I am going for a long walk, Naomi,' she said. 'I shall be home by tea-time.'

There was no fear of Naomi offering to accompany her stepmother. They had not walked together since Oswald Pentreath's departure. Day by day the gulf had been widening.

This walk of Cynthia's set Naomi wondering. Could she be gone to meet Oswald? That seemed of all things most unlikely. Joshua had the letter; it was Joshua who would keep the appointment. And then, O God! who would tell what might be the issue of the meeting!

Naomi went about the house and the garden like a wandering spirit for the next hour, and then it seemed to her that this suspense was beyond endurance; she must follow her father to the old shaft— she made very sure that he had gone there—she must be on the spot or near it, whatever harm was to come. O, why had she given him that shameful letter? Blind and wicked rage which prompted so wild an act!

'Did I want to make my father's life miserable, or to bring evil upon Oswald?' she cried. 'Yes, I was wicked enough for anything yesterday; I was mad with anger and jealousy.'

She put on her bonnet, and went out, unseen even by Sally, who was washing in the cool brick-floored back kitchen. The sun was blazing upon the neat little town. The white houses were of a dazzling brightness, the sweet-williams and red roses shone like spots of fire, the ruddy glow of the forge looked pale against the sun-glory. Naomi took no heed of the heat; she walked rapidly to the end of the lane that led to Matcherly, and then ran along the shaded narrow way till she came to the edge of the wood. Here she paused for a little, breathless and exhausted. They would be coming homewards by this time, she thought—Cynthia and Oswald, and he who had gone to watch their meeting—or to disturb it. She might come face to face with her false lover. Her heart beat wildly at the thought.

There was one central path through the wood, a

clearly defined cattle track, which she felt assured would be taken by any one going in the direction of the old shaft. It was easy to skirt this broad grassy track by a narrow footway that wound through the underwood, and among the smooth silvery beech boles and the rugged greenish-gray oak trunks. The path ran like a thread through the bracken. By this narrow way Naomi went swiftly, till she came to the rising ground that sloped upwards to Matcherly Common. Here she chose her post of espial behind a sturdy old oak, bearded with gray lichen and half strangled with ivy—a Methuselah of trees, from which Time had lopped limb after limb, but which still held numerous arms aloft, like a woodland Briareus, and seemed to threaten or denounce surrounding Nature. So one might fancy some prophetic Druid transformed into a tree, dumbly prophesying evil to come upon the earth.

Sheltered by this broad trunk, which stood waist high in hawthorn and bracken, Naomi waited to see her father and Oswald pass by, and to be assured that all was well with them. They would hardly fail to return by the cattle track; it was the only direct path to Combhaven, and on either side the underwood was too thick and wild for the perambulation of anything but the furred and feathered inhabitants of the forest.

She waited for what seemed a long and weary time; then, a little after four o'clock, she saw Cynthia go by, walking slowly. She was very pale, and the white wan cheeks bore the trace of tears; but she had a resigned look, as of one whose soul is not lost to peace.

'She has been to meet him,' thought Naomi. 'And yet she does not look like a shameless sinner.' Then she began to pray that Joshua might not have seen that clandestine unholy meeting—that he might have been spared the temptation to any evil act.

The time she had to wait for her father's coming hung heavily, so great had become that burden of nameless dread. Yet it was but half an hour after Cynthia had gone by that her husband came slowly along the forest glade, and passed within a yard of the tree behind which his daughter was watching.

She rose as he approached, and stood leaning

against the bulky old trunk, gazing at her father's face as she had never looked before at anything under God's heaven. Never had any other spectacle so thrilled, so frozen her being as this one view of a familiar countenance. To have looked in the face of the dead would have been less awful.

White to the lips, and with big drops of sweat upon brow and cheek, the mouth rigid, the dark eyes almost hidden under the lowering brows— Joshua, the Christian preacher, the man sure of election and grace, passed under the flickering lights and shadows, like some horrible vision of sin and vengeance—passed, and was gone. Naomi leaned against the tree, her hands clasped, her eyes gazing at the empty air, the shaft of afternoon sunlight upon which a million atoms, each a life, danced and sparkled; yet still seeing that blanched and awful face—the face of a man who had come straight from some hideous death-scene; the face of a man burdened with the secret of a crime.

'O God!' cried Naomi, with an overmastering despair, 'why didst Thou create us, predestined sinners, judged, doomed before we were born! The best of us, the most earnest, the truest, the noblest, given over a prey to the Evil One! My father, even my father, lowest, blackest of sinners!'

She stood in the same attitude, supported by the mossy trunk; stood as in a trance, and saw the sunlight dip lower behind the black branches and change from gold to rose, from rose to crimson, from deepest red to tenderest purple. She watched these changes in a kind of semi-consciousness and a strange feeling of uncertainty as to her own identity; this Naomi Haggard leaning against a tree seeming to her—the actual entity—to be a forlorn and stricken creature sorely to be pitied. She pitied herself and was sorry for herself with a half-scornful compassion. And so she waited, in a dreamy watchfulness, till nature gave way, and she sank, worn out, into a heap at the foot of the tree.

Here, faint and exhausted, but not unconscious, she still watched, till thick night came down upon the wood, and she heard the owls hooting and saw the rabbits running within a few feet of her resting-place. Only when the darkness closed round her did she rise and go home, too familiar with the wood to lose her way even amidst the shadows of night. She went homeward slowly, caring little who might question or wonder at her absence.

And in all the time of her watch she had not seen Oswald Pentreath go by.

CHAPTER V.

'AND YET I FEEL I FEAR.'

UNDER that quiet surface which life wore in Joshua Haggard's household there were troubled waters.

Naomi had never forgotten the awful look in her father's face that afternoon in the wood. It haunted her in all places and at all seasons. The impression it had made upon her mind would not pass away. What it meant she knew not—dared not shape the thought in her mind; but she was very sure that it meant evil of some kind—evil to her father's soul, wrong to Oswald.

If she could have known for certain that Oswald had carried out the intention set forth in his fatal letter to Cynthia, she would have been, comparatively speaking, at ease and happy. But of this she knew nothing. Whether he had really gone to America, how and when he had left Combhaven, of these things she was ignorant. Cynthia might know, perhaps; but not even to set these anxious fears at rest could Naomi stoop so low as to seek for any information about her lover from the woman for whose sake she had been abandoned. No; if Cynthia knew anything for certain, the knowledge must remain locked in her breast. Save in the merest outward and ceremonial form, a bare civility in every-day intercourse, there could be no contact between Naomi and her stepmother. The gulf that sundered these two was impassable.

Oswald's letter had stated that he meant to leave Combhaven by the night coach. He had not gone by that coach, for James Haggard, who was fond of an evening stroll when the shutters were up, and who took a lively interest in other people's business, had watched the departure of the coach on that particular evening, and entertained his family at the silent supper-table with a detailed account of that exciting event in the every-day life of his town.

'There was only one inside, and that was old Mrs. Skevinew, who is going to Exeter to see her married daughter,' said Jim; 'she had three bandboxes, two umbrellas, a pair of pattens, and a pair of the new-fashioned clogs—she bought 'em of aunt Judith the day before yesterday—a hamper of peas, a green goose, a basket of eggs, a tin of clouted cream, a red-cotton handkerchief full of bullaces, two pasties done up in brown paper, and a pig's head. Won't her friends be glad to see her?'

'Who were the outsides?' asked Judith.

Jim ran over the names, checking them off on his fingers.

'Was there no one else in the coach?' asked Naomi, looking at her father, who sat in his usual place with bent brows, neither eating nor drinking.

'No one.'

He had not gone by that coach, then, thought Naomi. But presently it occurred to her that Mr. Pentreath's return to Combhaven having been a secret and underhand proceeding, he would hardly care to leave the place under the broad glare of his townspeople's eye. The departure of the coach from the First and Last Inn was a public event. To leave by that vehicle at that point of departure, and not be seen, came hardly within the limits of possibility, unless a man had got himself hidden away in the boot before the spectators assembled. No, if Oswald had determined to travel by that coach, he had doubtless walked on to some quiet spot, to be taken up as the mail passed.

This reflection quieted Naomi's fears in some measure, yet did not set her heart at ease. Her father's face haunted her like some unholy image sent by Satan to suggest evil. What had passed between Joshua and that weak sinner—what violence of upbraiding had the minister used against his wife's lover? That there had been an angry meeting of some kind Naomi did not doubt. Only a wild indulgence of evil passion, only an utter abandonment of himself to man's omnipresent tempter, could have conjured up such a look in Joshua Haggard's face. The dark mind of the spirit of evil was there reflected. The lurid gleam in those darkly brooding eyes was the red glare caught from the open doors of hell.

There had been hard words spoken, words of hatred and fury, perchance even some act of open violence—a blow struck by that strong hand of Joshua's, who might have spurned the sinner as if he had been the tempter himself in his base form of serpent. But it was over, and Joshua had doubtless begun to repent of his violence; and Oswald was on his way to a distant world, to begin a new and wiser life.

'God keep him and guard him and lead him aright,' thought Naomi, 'and make him a good and great man. I could bear the pang of parting with him, could I feel secure about his happy future here and in the better world.'

O empty life from which he had vanished for ever! O dreary days which hung upon this young spirit like a burden, and weighed her down to the dust! Yes, verily, to the dust; so that, in her utter weariness, she felt as if it would be a good and pleasant end of all things to lie down in some lonely corner of the land—lie face downward among the fern and wild flowers, and wait for death. Surely the dark angel would take pity upon her joyless fate, and come and fold her in his sheltering wings, and comfort and cure her.

'There is no other comfort, no other cure,' she said, forgetting all the old pious lessons in her despair, forgetting even to do good to others in the sharpness of her pain.

She sought for consolation from no one—not even from honest Jim, who was distressed at seeing such blank hopeless faces in his home, and was eager, after his rough and ready fashion, to administer comfort.

'Come, Naomi, cheer up and be bright, like a sensible girl,' he would say. 'There's as good fish in the sea as ever came out of it, and though you've missed landing a fine salmon through father's foolishness, you'll have your net full by and by, I'll warrant. A good-looking straight-built lass like you will never want a sweetheart.'

'Jim, if you talk to me like that I shall hate you!' cried Naomi. 'I shall go single to my grave, and you know it; or if you can think otherwise of me, you're not worthy to be my brother.'

'Hoity-toity!' cried Jim, 'what fine notions run in our family! Here's father refusing the lord of the manor for his son-in-law, and you talking of dying an old maid because your first affections have been blighted. Why, if my first love takes a wrong direction, I shall turn my heart into the right road, as easily as I guide gray Dobbin down a lane where he doesn't want to go. Just a shake of the reins or a touch of the whip, and off we start.'

Crushed by this weariness of life, Naomi strove notwithstanding to do her duty. Even aunt Judith found no room for complaint with Naomi or Cynthia, unless haggard eyes and pale faces, and low voices with no joyous ring in them, were sufficient ground for upbraiding. The household work was faithfully performed. The starching and ironing, the dusting and beeswaxing, the sewing and darning were duly done. Cynthia had finished her dozen of shirts, without a gusset set awry, a seam puckered, or one deviation from a right line in the pearl-like stitching of collars and wristbands; and now she had taken to knitting Joshua's gray-woollen stockings, which was a pleasantly dreamy occupation calling for very little exercise of the intellectual faculties till one came to the heel. She used to sit in the garden or the wilderness in the calm September afternoons, with a grave quiet face bent over her flashing needles — a face that told of an abiding sorrow.

The Miss Weblings would scarcely have recognised their sunny-faced little maid in the serious young matron, with a complexion almost as white as her cap. Joshua rarely saw that patient figure sitting in his place on the grass-plat, for he had been growing more and more indefatigable in his visitations among the scattered members of his flock, walking great distances to lonely homesteads or labourers' cottages, or, when not thus occupied, spending his afternoons in solitary wanderings by the wild seashore, holding commune with his troubled soul.

Save at family prayer and at meals he was now seldom seen in his own house, while he had almost wholly deserted the shop. Aunt Judith bewailed this falling away from the good old habits which had made Haggard's the leading commercial institution in Combhaven. The salvation of one's soul was a vital transaction, doubtless; but a man secure of his calling and election in eternity could well afford to attend to his temporal business, instead of wandering about in desolate places like John the Baptist, without having any one to baptise.

'He might as well live on the top of a pillar like

St. Simon What's-his-name, and have his meals sent up to him by a ladder,' said Judith contemptuously, 'if his mind is never in his business. We're always running out of things now, for want of proper attention to the stock.'

To Naomi it was a small thing that her father should be indifferent to loss and gain, and turn his back upon the trade by which his father and grandfather had maintained their importance and respectability in the little town. The change she saw in him was more alarming than this neglect of daily duties—a change which she associated involuntarily with that bitter day on which she had seen his gloomy murderer's face pass by her in the woodland dimness.

In the autumn evenings, when she could escape from the joyless house, Naomi felt herself drawn, as by a magnet, to Pentreath Wood. It was not that she found peace there, or consolation. She loved the shadowy scene as a place in which she could feed her grief, and haunted it as an inconsolable mourner haunts the burial-ground where lies her dead. How desolate the place seemed in the season of earth's decay, all the winding ways deeply strewn with the red-brown leaves, soft and soddened in the hollows where the autumn rains lay longest; frogs croaking in the marshy places, and a dead snake lying here and there among the brambles!

It was not often that Naomi went within sight of the deserted house, where the old servants lived on in a lazy seclusion, waiting their master's bidding; almost as slumberous a household as that which slept for a hundred years in the old fairy story, only that here there was no lovely princess shining like a jewel in the innermost chamber of the castle. Here were only empty rooms and dust and loneliness.

One evening early in October, Naomi roamed a little farther than she had intended, and found that, to reach home in decent time, she must go by the nearest way, which was across the park, and out into the road by the park-gate. This would take her very near the house.

It was a fine bright evening. The sun had set redly behind the trees before she had entered the wood, and now the moon had risen and was shining over the great sea yonder—a lovely evening, mild and peaceful. She was loth to go back to the lighted room at home, and her father's evening lecture, now always of so gloomy a character as to minister to her despair rather than to lift up her soul from its depth of sorrow.

The hall-door stood open, and a light burned dimly within. Old Nicholas, the butler, was sitting in the porch. He recognised Naomi as she skirted the outer garden, and got up quickly and came after her.

'I beg your pardon, Miss Haggard, but seeing you go by just now, I made bold to follow you. Have you heard any news of the young Squire? I've wanted to ask sometimes when I've been up at the shop, to get my bit of tea and sugar; but your father wasn't about, and I don't like to ask your aunt—she's apt to be snappy.'

'No, Nicholas, we have had no news. You would be more likely to hear of your master than we.'

'Deary, now! I knew there was something wrong when he came down here so sudden, and told me I was to say nothing about it, and he was going off to Ameriky, and I was to keep the place in order agen Mr. Arnold came home, and then he was to be the master here. A power of changes to happen in such a short time, ain't it, miss? I feel as if the world was topsy-turvy, somehow. The poor old master gone! He was dreadful near, to be sure; but I'd got used to him, and I misses his fidgety pinching ways, looking after every candle-end, and such a nose of his own if he suspected we was frying a bit of bacon for supper. Well, he's gone where scraping and saving won't help him, poor gentleman. There's no candle-ends in the heavenly Jerusalem.'

Nicholas sighed despondently, as if he doubted whether an immortal home in which cheese-paring could not be practised would satisfy his departed master.

'And you haven't heard nothing, miss?'

'Nothing,' answered Naomi. 'But there is hardly time for any one to have had a letter yet, is there, Nicholas?'

'I can't say, miss. Perhaps not. It were the beginning of August when he went away, warn't it? and here we are in October. I suppose there wouldn't be time; and yet I begin to feel oneasy in my mind about him. There was something queer about his going away, you see.'

'How do you mean?' asked Naomi, looking at him intently.

'Well, you see, he says to me, "Nicholas, you get they two big trunks down to the coach this evening, and that there bag." The trunks was what he'd packed his clothes and books in, and suchlike, that morning, purpose to take them with him to Ameriky. "I shall walk on ahead, and let the coach pick me up this side of Henbury turnpike," he says. "But you get they trunks safe in the boot," says he. So the gardener and me puts 'em in a barrer and wheels 'em down, and gets 'em safe packed into the boot afore seven o'clock.'

'Well, what then?' asked Naomi, with suppressed eagerness.

'What then, Miss Haggard? Why, they trunks and that there bag is in the young Squire's room now—come back, like a bad penny!'

'Come back?'

'Yes. The coach never picked him up this side of Henbury turnpike. The coachman never set eyes upon him all along the road. When he got to Exeter, there was no one to take to they trunks, no directions left about 'em, so he just brought 'em back; and if the young Squire be gone to Ameriky, he be gone without his luggage. Lord, miss, how you do trimble! I hope there's nothing wrong, but it comes over me sometimes that things ain't altogether right.'

'He may have changed his mind at the last,' said Naomi falteringly. 'He may not have gone to America.'

'Perhaps not, miss; but wherever he's gone, he's gone without his luggage—even the carpet-bag, with his razors and night-clothes.'

'He may have had other luggage in London.'

'He had a black portmanteau at the inn where he'd been stopping in London, but it wasn't a big one. It wouldn't have been luggage enough for Ameriky, or anywhere else in foreign parts. And then the books and things that he was so fond of, and his writing-desk, and most of his clothes—all in they big boxes. It's odd he didn't send for 'em.'

'He may not want them.'

'But it's queer for him not to want 'em all this time. And if that there coach didn't pick him up—and we know it didn't—how did he get away? Nobody saw him leave, nobody heard of him. Lord-a-mercy, miss, how white you be! I didn't ought to say suchlike things, but it weighs so heavy on my mind, it's a comfort to talk about it. The London lawyer he sends me down my wages monthly, and board-wages for me and the others indoors. We might live on the fat of the land if we chose, only our constitutions have got used to pinching, and we likes it. We couldn't have a better place; only they two trunks weighs upon my mind, and I sha'n't feel easy till I've had a letter from my master.'

What comfort could Naomi give him—she whose thoughts were full of fear? She went home and found the family circle waiting for her. It was past the customary prayer-time by ten minutes or so.

'Rambling again, Naomi!' said her father severely; and then opened his Bible and began to read a chapter of Jeremiah, which he afterwards expounded, dwelling darkly on all that was darkest in the text. The prayer that followed was rather a cry of self-abasement and desolation than a supplicatory address, curiously different from that simple and single-minded appeal which the Divine Teacher dictated to His disciples. Joshua asked for no common wants of common life, he pleaded not to be forgiven as freely as he forgave ; but he grovelled in the dust before an angry God, and heaped ashes upon his head, and abased himself with humility which touched the confines of fanaticism.

'What kept you out so long, sis?' asked James, when they were seated at supper.

'Nicholas, the butler at the Grange, stopped me to ask about his master. He is very anxious about him.'

'Why?' asked her father sharply.

'Because he has been away so long, and has not written.'

Cynthia lifted her languid eyes, large with sudden terror.

'How could any one get a letter? He has not been gone three months. And even if there were time enough, why should he write to Nicholas?' said Joshua.

'Nicholas is anxious about him, in any case,' answered Naomi.

She said nothing about the luggage left behind, which was the chief cause of the old servant's uneasiness.

'Well, all I can say is, that a young man with such a property as that was a fool to go to America,' remarked Jim conclusively.

It was a generally accepted fact by this time that the young Squire had gone to America, and there were various versions of his motive for this exile. The male gossips inclined to the idea that he and Naomi had quarrelled, and that this lovers' quarrel had been the cause of his departure; the female portion of the community pinned their faith upon the young man's fickleness. He had repented of his engagement to the grocer's daughter, and had gone away to avoid its fulfilment.

'It was all very fine while his father was living, and likely to live to a hundred, and he hadn't a five-pound note,' said Mrs. Spradgers. 'He knew that Mr. Haggard was a warm man, and he might do worse than marry Naomi; but it was quite another thing when the old gentleman went off, and the property turned out better than young Mr. Pentreath had ever expected. It's only natural he should look higher. Circumstances alter cases.'

The year wore to its close, and yet there came no tidings of the young Squire. There was, perhaps, no reason why he should trouble himself to write to any one at Combhaven, argued Naomi, trying to shake off that burden of unquiet thoughts which oppressed her. He could hardly be expected to write to his old servants; he had provided for their comfort through his London solicitor. His rents were collected by a local agent and paid to the same man of business. There was no one at Combhaven who had any right to expect letters from him. He had broken away from his old moorings, and begun a new life in a new country. He was happy, perhaps, amused and interested by the novelty of his surroundings—occupied, adventurous, a light-hearted traveller, while her thoughts of him were so full of gloom.

'Why cannot I banish him from my mind altogether?' she asked herself. 'It is a sin to dwell thus persistently upon an earthly loss. "If thy right hand offend thee, cut it off." He came between me and heaven—for I loved him too well. Even now that he is far away the thought of him binds me down to earth. Why cannot I forget him?'

There was another question in her mind which hardly shaped itself in direct words: 'Why cannot I forget my father's face that day in the wood?'

The new year began, and there was no change in the quiet household, save a change in Cynthia which had been so gently wrought that it was invisible to the eyes that saw her daily. The minister's young wife had faded and drooped since that troubled summer time of the year just gone. The slender figure had lost its graceful curves, the white arm was no longer round and full, the oval of the cheek had fallen, and the blue-veined lids drooped languidly over the gentle eyes, in which there was a look that seemed to plead for pity or forgiveness.

Joshua's popularity was at its height this winter. Those stirring sermons—those eloquent theological fulminations—acted on his hearers as a stimulant and a tonic. People flocked to hear him from distant villages. He was proud of his popularity, lifted up and exalted by the idea that he was bringing sinners home to God, fighting hand to hand with the devil and all his angels. He lived apart from his own household, a stranger among them, though sitting by the same fireside. It was as if they were people of old time giving shelter to a prophet. They scarcely dared speak to him, but approached him with an awful respect. It was an understood thing that he had no more to do with the business which had in years past occupied half his time and some portion of his care. James now took the helm in the commercial vessel, and felt that he was of the stuff that makes great captains. Joshua seemed hardly aware of the change that had come over his life. He was a dreamer, and lived in a world of dreams.

So the year began, and it was early spring again, and Naomi felt that her youth was gone, and that the years could bring her nothing but age and death. They would come and go, and make no difference in her life. They held no promise, they knew no hope.

CHAPTER VI.

THE WANDERER'S RETURN.

It was March—just a year since the old Squire had been stricken with his fatal illness. The daffodils were blooming in sunny places; there was a faint tinge of green upon the hedgerows.

Naomi was sitting alone in the twilit parlour in the calm gray evening. She had done all her daily duties, and could afford to rest from her toil. She looked at the familiar scene—the glimpse of sea, the curve of the road winding up the hill towards Pentreath Grange—with sad hopeless eyes. No bright harbinger of joy would ever come to her by yonder road, down which she had seen the Squire's funeral train slowly descending with wind-tossed plumes and scarves less than a year ago.

'I had such a strange sense of loss that day,' she thought, remembering the dismal procession, and her own feelings as she watched its approach. 'I seemed to know that the end of my happiness had come; that change, or sorrow, or death was near.'

Twilight deepened, and the scene took a shadowy look. Who was this walking down the hill at a leisurely pace, with a careless easy gait which seemed familiar? Nay, it was familiar, for it set Naomi's heart beating vehemently; it made her cold and faint. This was no peasant returning from his work. She knew how the Combhaven population carried themselves. This tall slim figure, so straight, and yet so easy of motion, was no son of the soil, no hard-handed agricultural labourer, no fisherman smelling of tar and sea-weed, with wet raiment all glistening and scaly.

She stood up, and opened the window—stood with the chill March breeze blowing upon her terror-stricken face. This time she felt verily as if she were seeing a ghost.

'He has come back,' she thought. 'He is not dead. O foolish fear! O wretched doubt of the best and truest upon earth! He is safe; and has come back again. I shall see him once again, living and happy. My God, I thank Thee!'

The figure came nearer. Yes, it was Oswald Pentreath. She saw the well-remembered face in the dim light. How well he looked! how strong, how brave! Travel and strange countries had improved him. His chest had expanded, he walked with a firmer step, held his head higher. And he was coming to her father's house, boldly, with no stealthy approach. He came as a man who had done no evil, and had no cause for fear.

'He is cured of his folly; he is my true and noble lover once again. O God, Thou art full of mercy; Thy love aboundeth.'

The familiar figure was close at hand. There was nothing but the narrow front garden between him and Naomi; yet now there was a strangeness—her heart grew lead. The young man looked up at the house inquiringly, like a stranger who reconnoitres an unfamiliar place. He glanced up and down the street—quite empty of humanity at this moment, the solitary young woman with a basket, who had constituted its traffic a minute ago, having just gone indoors—then looked again at the house, and became conscious of Naomi's pale face at the window.

'I beg your pardon,' he began courteously. 'Is this Mr. Haggard's?'

Life-long sorrows are not so keen as a sudden stab like this—an arrow that pierces the heart and kills its hope for ever. It was not Oswald's voice. There was a likeness in the tone, that family resemblance so often to be found in the voices of kindred; but these tones were more decided, rougher. They lacked the poetic languor, the gentle sweetness of Oswald's utterance. This speaker was one who had commanded men on the high seas; not the musing idler who had wasted half his life lying listlessly in summer woods, or wandering with his rod beside autumn's swollen streams.

It was not Oswald. For the space of half a minute the surging blood in Naomi's brain almost blinded her. For an instant or so reason faltered, and she was on the verge of unconsciousness. Then the strong young soul resumed her power, and she comprehended that this was no shade from Avernus, but her lost lover's brother, the Squire's runaway son.

'Yes,' she answered, with a steady voice, 'this

is Mr. Haggard's house. Do you want to see my father?'

'Ah, then you are Naomi,' cried the stranger eagerly. 'I think I would rather talk to you than to your father; you can tell me more. I have only just come home, and I am very unhappy about my brother. May I come in, please?'

How friendly, how dear his voice sounded in its resemblance to the voice of Oswald! The familiar tones comforted Naomi somehow, after that bitter disappointment just now. Her heart was lifted up from its despair. Arnold had come home—Arnold would find out all about his brother.

At that thought a sudden dread came upon her, like a vision of doom.

If there were any guilty mystery in Oswald's fate, would not his brother bring the deed to light? Her shapeless fears rose up like gorgons and confronted her.

She opened the door for Arnold, and stood dumbly as he came in and held out his hand to her.

'How deadly cold your hand is!' he exclaimed 'I'm afraid I startled you coming so suddenly

People say I am very like my brother. And I daresay you are anxious about Oswald.'

He had gone into the parlour with her, and seated himself with a familiar friendliness close to the chair into which Naomi had sunk.

'Yes; I have been very anxious,' she said faintly.

'I can see that. Please God, there is no real cause for fear, though old Nicholas has frightened me a little by his raven-like talk. The last letter I had from my brother was written in London on the fourteenth of July. He urged me to come home, and told me he had some thoughts of going to America; and that if he went I was to take care of the estate in his absence, and to consider myself master, and so on, in his generous reckless way—as ready to give up all his privileges as Esau was to swop his birthright against a dish of lobscouse. This letter has been following me from port to port, and I only got it nine or ten weeks ago at Shanghai, where my ship was waiting for a cargo. I went straight to Oswald's London agent when I left the docks; but he could tell me nothing, except that my brother had made all arrangements for a long absence from England. He was to have sailed for New York on the fourteenth of August. But a thing that puzzled this lawyer fellow a little was that Oswald should have drawn no money since he left home. "He may have taken plenty with him," said I—for you see Oswald was brought up to make a little money go a long way, or to do without it altogether mostly. "So he may," said the lawyer; "but I find that young men generally do draw a good deal of money when they've got any sources to draw upon—and even, sometimes, when they have not. It's a way they have." This made me rather uneasy, and I came down here as fast as those blundering coaches, which hardly do six knots an hour, could bring me. And the old house looked so lonely and dismal without Oswald, that the mere sight of it made me miserable; and then old Nicholas's raven croakings made me worse; so I came straight off to you for comfort.'

'I can tell you nothing,' answered Naomi, with a sigh.

'Nicholas told me you had received no letter. That's strange, certainly. He would have written to you before any one, I should think.'

'No, I had no right to expect any letter from him. I expected none.'

'What—not as his betrothed wife?'

'Our engagement was broken off some time before he went. Did you not know?'

'Not a word. His last mention of you was full of affection—not in his latest letter, by the way, but in the one which told me of my father's death. I was to come home, and be very fond of you, and we were all to be happy together.'

'Yes, I know,' said Naomi, with a pang of bitterest remembrance. How often had Oswald talked to her of union and love and happiness—sweet domestic joys which Arnold was to share!

'But why was your engagement broken off?' asked the sailor bluntly. 'Did you quarrel?'

'Quarrel? No.'

'He must have behaved very ill, then.'

'No, no. It was my father's wish. I obeyed my father in setting Oswald free. And he accepted his liberty—he was grateful for his release. Love does not always last a lifetime: there is a difference, you see. I think that he once loved me, but—'

Here the tears rained down upon her trembling hands. Arnold drew nearer to her, and gently pressed one of those cold hands with a brotherly kindness.

'My poor girl—my sister that was to have been! He behaved badly, I'm afraid. There was something wild and mysterious in his last letter; and then that sudden resolve to go to America! I ought to have seen that things had gone wrong with him. Poor Oswald! And I expected to see him so happy with you.'

'Providence willed it otherwise. I was too happy with him, I think—too much absorbed in the joys of this world.'

'Why should we not be happy in this world? God would never have made so fair a world for a scene of suffering. You can't imagine, you stay-at-home people, how beautiful this earth is. The birds and animals and reptiles and insects are happy. All free creation enjoys itself, from its birth to its death. Why should man be wretched, or the source of misery in others? Why should Providence be offended because you and my brother loved each other and were happy?'

Naomi could not answer. It was an article of her religion that Heaven disapproved of too much earthly bliss.

'But you must have known where he was going—he told you his plans, surely?' asked Arnold.

'No, I knew nothing of his intentions—directly,' answered Naomi, a faint blush dyeing her pallid cheek.

'Did you not see him when he came back to the Grange in the beginning of August? He came to bid you good-bye, I suppose?'

'No, I did not see him.'

'Then why did he come back to Combhaven at all? I can hear of nothing that he did in the way of business, except to pack those trunks, which he left behind him after all his trouble. What was the motive of his return?'

'Indeed, I cannot tell you,' faltered Naomi, sorely distressed.

Arnold looked troubled. He rose and walked up and down the narrow parlour, as he had walked his quarter-deck in many an hour of doubt and difficulty.

'I can't understand it,' he said. 'It is the strangest business altogether. Why did he come back and pack his trunks, and have them taken to the coach, and why did he not appear to claim them? If he did not leave by the coach, how did he get away?'

'There are vessels that sail between Rockmouth and Bristol, are there not?' suggested Naomi. 'He may have gone that way.'

'A slow roundabout way for him to choose, after making up his mind to go by the coach. I begin to feel as anxious as Nicholas. O my dearest Oswald, where are you, and why this mystery? God grant that he is safe and happy somewhere! God grant there has been no foul play!'

At these words Naomi's face took a deathlike hue. But the room was too dark for Arnold to see the change.

'If harm of any kind has happened to him, Heaven help the wrongdoers, for they shall have no mercy from me! I'll hunt them down. But no, I won't think it. I won't believe that he has come to an untimely end—the brother who carried me in his arms, and was so gentle and loving, and whom I loved, God knows, with all my heart, though I left him! How I have looked forward to our reunion, and counted upon it, and built upon it in all these years! And I come back to find him far away, and his fate a mystery.'

He threw himself into a chair and sobbed aloud, honest manly tears coming from a loyal heart.

It was Naomi's turn to be comforter. She bent over him, and laid her hand lightly on his shoulder.

'Pray do not say that evil has befallen him,' she said. 'He may have changed his mind as to his way of travelling at the last; who can tell what trifling thing may have influenced him?'

'What did he do with himself all that day?' asked Arnold. 'Nicholas tells me that he left the Grange before one o'clock, and the coach was not to pick him up till after eight in the evening. Where was he? With whom did he spend his time? He seems to have no friends in Combhaven but you and your family. And he was not with you?'

'No.'

'Cannot you help me to find out where he was?'

'No, I cannot.'

'That's a pity. If I could only find out the people who saw the last of him here, they might enlighten me as to his intentions. I must see what I can do elsewhere. I came to you naturally for help; but then I did not know your engagement was broken off.'

Sally brought in the lighted candles, and started at sight of the sea-captain.

'Don't be frightened, Sally,' said Naomi; 'this is Captain Pentreath, the Squire's brother.'

'Lor' sakes!' faltered the handmaiden, 'I took he for the young Squire's ghost.'

'Is your father at home?' asked Arnold presently; 'I should like to see him.'

'No, it is his class-night; he will not be home for nearly an hour. And I know he could tell you nothing more than I have told you,' added Naomi.

'Perhaps not, but he might advise me; I have heard that he is a superior man. I should like to see him: I'll call to-morrow. Good-night, Naomi— I may call you Naomi, I hope, for my brother's sake? He told me to think of you as a sister.'

'I should like you to think me so still, if you can,' Naomi answered gently.

And then he pressed her hand, and was gone.

There was some kind of comfort in the sailor's friendliness, in this brave, strong, manly figure suddenly introduced into the dull scene of a sorrow-shadowed life. He was so like Oswald, and yet so unlike. And he loved his brother so dearly. Oswald's fate would be no longer a mystery. All those unspoken fears, which had preyed upon her like a consuming disease, would be proved vain and foolish. He was safe, he was happy in some strange land. There needed only a little energy and cleverness to find out all about him, and Arnold would supply both.

Then there flashed upon her the memory of that awful moment in the wood, when she saw her father go by with a look upon his face that seemed to her like the brand of Cain, full of awful meaning.

CHAPTER VII.

'WHERE IS THY BROTHER?'

'FATHER,' said Naomi at supper-time, 'Captain Pentreath has come home, and wants to see you to-morrow.'

'Captain Pentreath!' echoed Joshua, staring at her blankly; 'who's he?'

'Oswald's brother.'

'O, Arnold, the younger son, the boy who ran away to sea? He's come home, has he, to take possession of the estate? That's a good thing.'

'Not to take possession, father; to take care of the old place, perhaps. He has no right to take possession in his brother's lifetime.'

'Not unless he had stayed away seven years without being heard of,' interjected Jim, the English mind having a firm grip upon this idea of seven years.

'Why should any one suppose him dead?' asked

Naomi, with a look that was half indignant, half apprehensive; 'he has only been away a little more than six months. His brother has come home to look for him. He is determined to find him.'

'What's the use of looking for him at Combhaven, when everybody knows he's gone to America?' cried Jim.

'I mean that Captain Pentreath is going to find out all about his brother—when and how he left England.'

'Poor worm!' exclaimed Joshua, with lofty scorn. 'His brother's fate is in the hands of God. As if he could make or mend it!'

'But he has a right to know, father, and it is natural he should be anxious.'

'That shows he belongs to the unregenerate,' said Jim, glad to have a fling at the creed which had been forced upon him before he was able to form his own estimate of its merits, like vaccination. 'If he were sure of his own election, he needn't care a toss what became of his brother—'

'In time, perhaps not,' said Joshua, with an awful look; 'but how dreadful to know him lost in eternity! Better to remain for ever ignorant of the fate of those we love than to be sure of their condemnation.'

'Judge not, that ye be not judged,' said Naomi, for the first time in her life daring to lift up her voice against her father. 'Who can be sure of another's condemnation? It is blasphemy to say such a thing.'

'What new Daniel is this?' exclaimed Joshua scornfully. 'Is my daughter going to be my teacher? I tell you, Naomi, there are some sins which cannot be repented of. There is a guiltiness which seals the sinner's doom, and sends him self-convicted to receive his Maker's sentence.'

'I have no fear that Oswald would be such a sinner,' answered Naomi, meeting her father's dark look with defiant eyes. 'Weak, erring, led astray by one more erring than himself—yes, he might be these; but not a deliberate offender, not obstinately guilty.'

What was this new feeling which made her talk to her father as if she was arguing with an adversary? She felt a thrill of horror at her own audacity. But she was not mistress of herself when her father spoke harsh words of Oswald Pentreath. Reason grew clouded and the voice of passion cried aloud in defence of her lost lover. He was weak, and she would not let the strong man spurn him. He was absent, and she would not hear him condemned.

Cynthia sat silent, and heard them talk of the man who had loved her too well, whose only sin was to have let his heart go out to her as a young bird flies from its nest into the glad new world. He had loved her, and that love had darkened his life. She could see him looking down at her, as on that last day, passion-pale breathing his eternal farewell. What a dream it had been—so fair, so sweet, so unreal! She had suffered herself to be beloved, and to love again, and in this dreaming half-unconscious state had tasted an ineffable happiness. She did not regret this lost dream-world; she would not have recalled its vanished sweetness; she was honestly repentant of her sin against the husband she honoured; but the past was ineffaceable—a part of her being.

> ' I cannot but remember such things were
> That were most precious to me.'

Though full of anxious thoughts, Arnold Pentreath brought brightness and pleasant days to the old Grange and all who came within his influence. His candid intelligent face, the frank heartiness of his manners, with just a dash of the seaman's bluntness, and that firm straightforwardness which comes from the habit of commanding others and restraining oneself—all these things gave him immediate mastery over the simple folks at Combhaven. The old servants worshipped him. In boyhood he had been the more daring and mischievous of the two brothers, and naturally the more popular. He had defied his old father, and had won golden opinions from the household by his juvenile mutinies. He came back a man, broad-shouldered and strongly built, bronzed by tropical suns and hard weather, but all the handsomer, in the eyes of a sea-loving population, for his sunburnt cheek and the stubborn crispness of his hair. He was fonder of his fellow-men than Oswald had been, and, instead of dreaming over *Childe Harold* in Pentreath Wood, was out and about all day, tramping along the lanes, making acquaintance with every hind who worked upon his land, tossing cottage children in his strong arms, with a kindly word for every one he met.

He had not been three days at the Grange before the fact of his return was known far and wide, and brought all manner of applicants to the old house to ask favours which no agent would grant. He heard all complaints with an equable good-nature, and lent his attention to the smallest detail: the slates blown off the homestead in 'they high winds—now do 'ee see what 'ee can do for us, Squire.' The granary thatch which had 'cotched fire' in such a mysterious way after last midsummer's thunderstorm, that old Farmer Westall was firmly convinced it was the work of Nancy Dowben, the witch.

'For she be a witch, Squire,' said the farmer, 'that's well beknownst. And I do say as it ain't right a spiteful old 'ooman like she should be allowed to have the handling of forked lightning.'

'Well, farmer, if it was witchcraft fired the barn, you can't expect me to pay for new thatching it?' argued Arnold.

'But look 'ee now, Squire. It was the ould gentleman, your feyther, brought it on us. All they witches bore an evil eye towards him. He were so hard upon 'em, and that screwy, never a drop of milk or a fagot to give 'em.'

'Wasn't it you, now, that refused old Nancy the fagots, Farmer Westall?' suggested Arnold.

'Well, now, you're a bit of a conjuror yourself, Squire. There was one day as the ould 'ooman come for some wood to bile her kittle, and I wasn't in the best of tempers, for our ould sow had etten up seven pegs, and I thowt it was some o' Nancy's work; so I calls out, "Now jist look yere, Nancy; you had a fagot yesterday, and another the day afore that, and I didn't make that stack o' wood o' purpose for you, old lady." So she gives a sniff and a grunt, and off she goes; and it wasn't a week from that when the lightning caught the thatch of my biggest barn. And I'm a man with a long fambly, Squire, and I've had the roof covered up anyhow some old boards and a bit of tarpaulin ever since, because Bill Stowell, the thatcher, asks a mort o' money before he'll make a good job of it.'

'We'll see what can be done, farmer. Perhaps

I might go halves in the expense, if the barn was roofed in to my satisfaction. I'm only a steward, you see—a kind of deputy for my brother.'

Farmer Westall sighed and looked glum. Old Nicholas, the butler, had infected most of his acquaintance with his own dismal ideas about the absent lord of the manor. It was a general opinion that the vessel in which Oswald had sailed for America had gone to the bottom.

'There are some folks that'll never get no luck out o' the sea,' said the voice of public opinion as represented by the fishermen of Combhaven. 'Remember that storm, and the way the Dolphin went to pieces. The two sailors was saved easy enough, but the Squire would have been drownded or knocked to pieces on they rocks but for Joshua Haggard. And what were the use of saving him? He never did no good to the Haggards; and here he is gone down to the bottom, as sure as fate. It was what were meant from the fust, and there's never no good in flying in the face of Providence. You may save a ship's cargo—that's man's business—and an honest way of purvidin' for a fambly; but they as is aboard the ship is in the care o' Providence, and it's clear blasphemy to risk your life in fishing of 'em out o' the water!'

Captain Pentreath had exhausted his resources, and had found no clue to his brother's proceedings after that August noontide in which he had left the Grange, with the avowed intention of going to Exeter—on his way to London—by the evening coach. Arnold had gone back to London, and had seen the solicitor again, and had made his inquiries in every likely and unlikely direction, but he had learned nothing. The London lawyer did not know the name of the vessel in which Oswald had booked his passage to New York. His client had told him nothing, except that he had made up his mind to go to America, and that he wanted his affairs administered in his absence. The household at the Grange was to suffer no alteration, and when Arnold came he was to be master.

'Until your return!' the lawyer had said to him.

'My return is an event of the remote future,' Oswald had replied; 'I may never return.'

Arnold went to Liverpool, and the result of his researches there convinced him that Oswald had not left that port in any vessel bound for America, unless he had sailed under an assumed name. From Liverpool he went to Cork—from Cork he went by water to Bristol—from Bristol westward to Plymouth; and the most searching inquiries at these places resulted as his inquiries had resulted at Liverpool. There was no trace of Oswald Pentreath's passage to America to be found in any shipping office. He went back to the Grange sorely depressed, for his brother's fate was beginning to assume a hue of mystery which gave room for the darkest fears.

His conversation with Joshua Haggard had told him nothing more than he had already learned from Naomi. The minister had received him with a chilling reserve. The frank outspoken sailor wondered that his brother could have written to him so warmly in praise of such a man.

He called on Joshua again on the day after his return from his round of inquiry.

'This is a bad business, Mr. Haggard,' he began, plunging at once into the subject nearest his heart;

'I have found out enough to feel very sure that my brother has not gone to America.'

Joshua's grave countenance betrayed no surprise. 'Why, the fellow is not a man but a machine!' Arnold thought indignantly.

'You don't seem to understand what a serious question this is,' said Arnold. 'If my brother did not go to America last August, what has become of him?'

'That is a question which I cannot be expected to answer, Captain Pentreath. We are all in God's hands. In life or in death He deals with us as seemeth best to Him. He may have appointed your brother for an evil end. You had best be content to leave all to Him.'

'Do you mean that if my brother has come to an evil end I am to let his murderer go scot-free?' cried Arnold indignantly. 'Do you think that I shall fold my hands and wait for Providence to avenge my brother? Why, if I did, God would have the right to ask of me as he did of Cain, "Where is thy brother?" You do not know how dearly we two loved each other, Mr. Haggard.'

'"Vengeance is mine; I will repay,"' quoted Joshua solemnly; 'be sure that if your brother has been murdered, an idea I do not for a moment entertain, his assassin has suffered or will suffer as heavy a punishment as any vengeance of yours could inflict.'

'May God make conscience an undying worm to feed upon his soul!' said Arnold. 'But it shall be my business to bring his body to the gallows.'

Joshua heard him in silence. He sat with folded hands, and a countenance as mysterious in its solemn thoughtfulness as the head of Memnon.

'Come, Mr. Haggard, you must be able to give me some help in this matter, if you choose,' urged Arnold passionately; 'my brother was your daughter's lover—her affianced husband, till you, for some motive of your own, forbade their marriage. There is a story underlying that act of yours—a story that might cast some light upon my poor brother's fate. You must have had strong reasons for such a step. A man of your principles would hardly be governed by caprice. Tell me honestly what that reason was. Remember I have a right to ask.'

'I can give you no details upon that point,' answered Joshua, after some moments of profound thought, 'but I will tell you broadly that I had reason to disapprove of your brother's conduct in relation to another woman. I had reason to know that his heart had gone away from my daughter. He would have kept his promise, and married her, and would have believed that he was acting as a man of honour; but he would have lied at God's altar, and his marriage would have offended Heaven.'

'You believe that my brother's heart had gone astray?'

'I know it.'

'Then, for Heaven's sake, tell me all you know. This love-affair may throw light upon his after conduct—may give us the clue to his present whereabouts. There would be a false delicacy—an absolute cruelty—in hiding anything from me—from me, his brother, who am distracted by the most hideous apprehensions.'

'I can tell you nothing more,' answered Joshua, with a stern resoluteness which chilled Arnold to the heart. 'I am withholding no knowledge which could help you in the smallest degree. Your brother sinned—and is gone. You must be content to know no more than that.'

'I will not be content!' cried the sailor vehemently. 'You are juggling with me — you, a preacher of God's Word, who ought to be truthful as the day! But I forgot—the prophets were dark of speech, and God taught His chosen people by dreams and allegories, and you seek to imitate those mysterious ways. Have you no human pity—as a man and a Christian—for a brother's grief for a lost brother? You could tell me something that would make this mystery clear; and you lock your lips, and abandon me to the agony of uncertainty. My brother respected, admired—nay, loved you, Mr. Haggard.'

This wrung a sigh from a breast which Arnold had deemed marble.

'I tell you I am withholding nothing that could give you comfort,' said Joshua, looking downward with gloomy brow. 'I deplore your brother's fate, and the mystery which surrounds it. Yet for your

sake—for the sake of my daughter who loved him—
I say, May the veil never be lifted!'

'Why?'

'Because I fear he came to a bad end.'

'You must have some reason for that fear. You know something!' exclaimed Arnold breathlessly.

'I am guided by my knowledge of his character—of his condition of mind last summer.'

'You think he destroyed himself?'

'I do.'

Arnold bowed his face upon his clasped hands; his strong frame was shaken by the agony of that moment. To have stayed away from his brother all the days of his youth—to come home full of hope and pleasure—and to be told this! The cup was bitter.

When Arnold looked up, Joshua Haggard was gone.

He stayed in the empty room, looking out into the windy street—where one old woman was tightening a three-cornered shawl across her skinny shoulders—with eyes that saw not, and thinking over Joshua's words.

What did they mean? How much, or how little?' Was this idea of Oswald's suicide a mere speculation on the minister's part, or had he sound evidence on which to found his conclusions?

'It is too bad of him to leave me in the dark,' mused Arnold. 'I have a right to know everything that can be said or thought about my brother. He is a hard-hearted scoundrel. These over-pious men are adamant. And yet he saved my brother's life at the risk of his own. Oswald told me the story, and the fishermen here are never tired of talking about it. Don't let me forget that. The man is better than his speech. And he tells me he is keeping nothing back. But to think that my brother took his own life—that he was wretched enough to find the coward's last release from difficulty! I will not believe it.'

He rose to depart; but before he got to the door, Naomi came in, and they stood face to face, both startled, both agitated by this sudden meeting, natural as it was.

'O Naomi, I want you,' cried the sailor, taking both her hands, and looking into the pale face with beseeching earnestness. 'I want you to advise, to comfort, to enlighten me. I have been talking to your father, and he has almost broken my heart. Tell me, for pity's sake, the truth, dear, as sister to brother. Say that you do not believe Oswald killed himself.'

'Killed himself?' she echoed, growing very white. 'No. Who says so—who thinks so?'

'Your father.'

'My father says that—my father believes that?'

'Yes, dear. He told me so five minutes ago. Only say that you don't believe it.'

'I do not!' she answered, with flashing eyes. 'I know that he was unhappy, but I cannot believe—I will not believe—that he could be so weak—so guilty. No, there was no such thought in his mind. He had made his plans for beginning a new life; he had taken his passage for America.'

'You know that from himself?' cried Arnold eagerly.

Naomi bowed her head in assent.

'God bless you, sister!' said the sailor. 'You

have comforted me more than I can say. You knew him—you loved him.'

'With all my heart and soul—too much for duty, or peace, or righteousness.'

'And you think he really did go to America?'

Naomi's troubled face took a still deeper shadow.

'I know he meant to go.'

'Yet it was strange that he should not have left by the coach, after telling Nicholas that he meant to go that way. Very strange that he should leave those trunks behind him after packing them.'

'He may have changed his mind at the last. He was troubled in mind, and might be careless about things which people in an ordinary state of mind would consider important.'

'True, my dear. How clearly you see everything! Yes, that was so. And he sailed from some small port, perhaps—or from the other side of the Channel, Havre or Brest. The fact that I cannot trace him signifies nothing. We will wait and hope, Naomi; hope for your husband and my brother's return.'

'For our brother's return,' answered Naomi, with a tender gravity. 'He can never again be more to me than a brother: and to the end of my life I shall love him with a sister's love.'

'Poor fellow!' said Arnold dreamily; 'he threw away a jewel above all price when he lost you.'

CHAPTER VIII.

THE FACE IN OSWALD'S SKETCH-BOOK.

That idea of his brother's suicide took no strong hold upon Arnold after his conversation with Naomi; but he could not put the possibility out of his mind altogether. That his brother had suffered some disappointment—that a cloud of some kind had darkened his life—he was ready to believe. Oswald's latest letter had betrayed a mind ill at ease; that sudden determination to leave his country, while independence was still a new thing for him, and with every advantage in life that could make a young man happy, argued the existence of some deep-rooted sorrow, a misery that made familiar scenes hateful, and exile a welcome means of escape from the haunting memories that follow a fatal passion.

But, having resolved upon exile, could Oswald have been so weak or so wicked as to seek the darker and more desperate Lethe of the suicide? Arnold argued that his brother was too good and brave a man to contemplate, much less to commit, such a crime. But then Arnold had not read *Werther*, the apotheosis of suicide.

He went back to the Grange, after his interview with Naomi, more than ever at sea as to his brother's fate, more than ever resolved to unravel the mystery. His first act was to make an inquiry which had some bearing upon the suicide question. Instead of entering the Grange by the hall-door, he went under the old stone archway that led into the quadrangle, from which the kitchens and stables alike opened, being tolerably certain of finding Nicholas the butler sunning himself on the solid old bench beside the kitchen-door.

There sat the old man, bare-headed, basking in the spring sunshine. It did not last very long, the sunshine of these April afternoons; but while it lasted there was warmth and a balmy sweetness in the air, and a yellow light that made all things lovely. The wallflowers blended their rich red and gold with the cool grays and purples of the old stone archway, the dark-brown shadows on stable-doors and deep-set windows, the vermilion lights upon the tiled roofs. The stonecrop on the gables, the sage-green houseleeks nestling round the disused chimney-stacks, the fleecy clouds sailing high in a bright blue sky, were all beautiful to contemplate, but such familiar objects to the drowsy eye of old Nicholas, stretching out his feeble legs in the warmth as he stretched them towards the kitchen-hearth indoors, that he was scarcely conscious of their existence. If he had an idea at all about the old quadrangle, it was that all 'they' wallflowers, and houseleek, and stonecrop, and rubbish ought to be swept away, and the whole place renovated with a coat of clean whitewash.

He was puffing slowly at his afternoon pipe when Arnold came up; but at the sight of his master he rose and did obeisance.

'Sit down, Nicholas, and go on with your pipe,' said the sailor, in a friendly voice; 'I want a little quiet talk with you.'

The butler obeyed, and Arnold seated himself on the bench by his side, and took out a short German pipe, which he carried in his pocket, and began to smoke. It was in the days when a German pipe was a mark of a traveller, when for a gentleman to smoke a pipe of any kind implied a republican turn of mind.

Captain Pentreath looked round the quadrangle. There was no one within earshot. The stable-boy was throwing a pail of water at Herne's hind legs at the furthest end of the yard—a liberty which the animal bore with the resignation engendered of custom. Two fantail pigeons were puffing out their chests and spreading out their fans on the deep red tiles yonder; and a most vagabond collection of poultry was disporting itself on a golden mountain of straw in a distant corner—a mountain which would have made the old Squire wild with agony had he seen such a wasteful expenditure of litter; but Herne's bed nowadays was a Sybarite's couch, Arnold having taken his brother's horse under his own especial protection.

'You remember the day my brother went away the last time, Nicholas; the day you got his trunks taken down to the coach-office?'

'Yes, Captain; as well as if it was yesterday.'

' Did you see him just before he left the house?'

' Yes; he called me into the hall as he was going out to give me his last orders about they trunks.'

' Do you know if he carried pistols? There was a pair used to hang over the mantelpiece in his bedroom. I've noticed the mark of them on the wall where the panelling has changed colour. Do you know if he took them with him?'

' Yes, Captain. I saw the butt-end of a pistol poking out of his breast-pocket. He wore a frock-coat buttoned up tight, and there was just the end of the pistol showing. They was pretty little pistols, as small as tyes, and he was uncommon proud of 'em. They'd belonged to his great uncle, the Colonel, you see; and was furrin made. "You beant going to carry they pistols, be ye, Squire," said I, for I thought it was dangerous. But he said he wanted to take the pistols away with him, and he'd forgot to pack 'em in his box. "And perhaps it's as well," he says; "for it beant wise to go on a coach journey without firearms;" and I says, "Lawks, master Oswald," for I forgets myself sometimes with un, and thinks he's still a bye, "you ain't afeard o' highwaymen in these days, be ye, with the reform bill a-comin' to make things pleasant to everybody?" But he on'y larfed, and shuk his head, and went out without another wurred.'

'With a pair of pistols in his breast-pocket,' thought Arnold, much disturbed by this information, for it seemed to jump with Joshua Haggard's idea of self-slaughter. He asked no further questions of old Nicholas, but went slowly to his own room—the large airy bedchamber, with windows facing seaward, which had been Oswald's—and sat down at his brother's writing-table, to meditate upon the mystery that veiled the absentee's fate.

That there was a mystery of some kind Arnold was fully assured. It was now high time that somebody in England should have heard from the wanderer. The brothers had corresponded more or less regularly in all the years of their separation, and Oswald had always been the best correspondent. The landsman had made excuses for the rover when Arnold's letters were in arrear, and had written by every mail, so that Captain Pentreath often found a packet of letters waiting for him when his ship came into port, full of pleasant gossip about the old home which he dearly loved, although he loved the sea better. That Oswald should be away nearly a year, living, and in his right mind, and in all that time make no communication with his brother, seemed improbable to the verge of impossibility.

'Where did he go when he left the Grange that August day?' pondered Arnold. 'Some one must have seen him; some one must know something about him. The woman he loved—for whose sake he jilted that noble girl—she could give me the clue to the mystery, perhaps, if I only knew where to find her.'

Who was she? Who was the object of that fatal passion which had darkened Oswald's life just when it seemed happiest? Arnold wondered exceedingly. Some one his brother had known in London, perhaps; for it could hardly be any one at Combhaven without every one in the place knowing all about it; and the people who talked to Arnold about his brother were clearly quite in the dark as to the reason of his falling away from his allegiance to Naomi. No, it could be no one at home, or he would have heard of it at the street-corners; and yet it was evident to him that Joshua Haggard knew more about the circumstances of Oswald's sin or folly than he cared to tell. He had known enough to feel justified in breaking off his daughter's engagement—a strong measure, assuredly, where Naomi had so much to gain by the intended marriage. How had Oswald's conduct in London reached the Methodist minister's knowledge? That was puzzling. But even the remotest village has generally some channel of communication with the great city—some curious rustic, who has a brother or cousin living within sound of Bow bells, and is occasionally gratified by his city friend with a dish of scandal. No latest rumour, or darkest insinuation about courts or princes, so interesting to Mr. Chawbacon as the news of his brother parishioner's doings 'up in London.'

There stood Oswald's two big trunks in the deep recess by the chimney, one on the top of the other, just as they had been placed when the coach brought them back from Exeter. Might not one of these hold a clue to their owner's intentions when he left his home? Arnold had his sea-going tool-chest close at hand. He had a good deal of mechanical skill, and had always rigged up his own cabin, with the book-shelves and three-cornered brackets and small conveniences that give a comfortable and civilised air to an apartment which, to the landsman's eye, looks like an exaggerated rabbit-hutch.

Arnold had picked the lock of the topmost trunk before he had time to reason upon his idea. It was an old leather-covered trunk of his father's; black with age, and iron-clamped at the corners, and so heavy in itself that it was a matter of comparative indifference to the person who carried it whether it was full or empty. Arnold lifted the lid with a curiously nervous feeling, as if some sudden and appalling revelation were lurking immediately beneath it.

This uppermost trunk contained Oswald's modest collection of books—the well-thumbed Shakespeare and Byron, the queer little duodecimo *Tom Jones* and *Joseph Andrews*. Arnold took them up one by one, and looked at them tenderly. He too was a worshipper of that poetic star so lately set, and carried *Childe Harold* and *Don Juan* in his sea-chest, and had sat dreaming over their pages many a night, with no other light to read by than the broad tropical moon; he too was a lover of Shakespeare and Fielding. He turned over the leaves of that battered old Byron meditatively, and it seemed to him that the volume opened at the saddest passages, as if the reader had dwelt with morbid fondness upon the complainings of a kindred despair.

Below the books there was an old leather writing-desk, and below that nothing but clothes and boots, packed with a careless roughness, which indicated haste or preoccupation of mind on the part of the packer. In all the contents Arnold saw nothing that tended to his enlightenment, and he began to replace the things, putting them in carefully, with an orderly closeness of arrangement which reduced their bulk considerably.

He put in the books one by one, and had nearly finished his task, when his attention was caught by a shabby little volume without any title on the back, which had hitherto escaped his notice. It was bound in red morocco, and had grown dingy from much usage.

Arnold opened the book. It was a manuscript book, containing entries in Oswald's penmanship, alternated with pencil-sketches, and here and there a few verses, with much interlineation and alteration, to denote the throes of composition.

'This must tell me something,' thought the sailor.

The pencil revealed the tastes of the owner of the little volume. The first pages were full of marine sketches, pencil dottings of familiar bits of coast. They brought back the memory of Arnold's boyhood—those old days when his chief delight was to get on board one of the fishermen's boats, and to be out at sea from dawn to sunset; or, better still, from sunset to sunrise. He had offended his father many a time by these unauthorised excursions; and his final offence had been an absence of three days and nights at the beginning of the pilchard season. He had come home and begged pardon for his wrongdoing; but the Squire, who had suffered some pangs of paternal anxiety for the first time in his life, resented this trifling with his finer feelings, and gave the truant a ferocious flogging. Whereupon the sea-loving scapegrace made up his bundle, and set out after dark to walk to Bristol.

It was fifteen years since he had seen these picturesque bits of coast—Clovelly and Hartland Point, and the remoter glories of Bude and Tintagel. Yes, every angle of cliff, every jagged rock, brought back the fervour and freshness of his boyhood, the days when his love of the sea was a worship, and not merely a professional ardour.

There was the Dolphin, pitching and rolling in heavy seas, or mirrored in summer lakes of sultry calm. There were a good many attempts at versification in this earlier part of the book, all savouring of Byron; addresses to 'My Barque;' invocations to storm and ocean, all unfinished.

Here, about midway in the volume, comes a woman's face—Naomi Haggard. Yes, although the likeness is by no means perfect, there is no mistaking the noble brow, the dark deep eyes with their look of thought, the masses of dark hair. This face was repeated many times—the heavy eyelids drooping, the full eyes lifted—in profile, three-quarter, full front; and now the poetic effusions took a bolder flight, and it was no longer the sea, but his mistress, the lover apostrophised. 'To N.' the verses were sometimes headed, or 'Midnight, after leaving N.' First love rang the changes in tenderest gushes of sentiment. All the old platitudes, the stock comparisons, were brought out, and the conventional Pegasus was duly exercised. He was not a winged horse, to soar over the topmost pinnacle of Parnassus, but a quiet cob rather, warranted easy to ride and drive, a steed that took his rider over familiar ground at a gentle trot, and never showed the slightest inclination to bolt with him.

The middle of the book was entirely filled with sketches of Naomi and verses to Naomi, and here and there a faint murmur against Naomi's coldness jotted down in prose. Then came a change: Naomi disappeared altogether; there were no more poetic efforts, but page after page closely written—a journal, evidently, kept from day to day. The earliest date was in the March of the previous year.

And now appeared a face which was unknown to Arnold; a girlish face, in a Puritan cap, delicately traced, as if the lightest touch of the draftsman's pencil had not been fine enough to mark the ethereal character of his subject. Sweet face—now grave, now pensive, now touched with a vague melancholy, now with deepest sadness in the tender uplifted eyes—eyes that seemed to pity and deplore.

'This is the woman he loved,' thought Arnold. He turned to the diary, and read a page at random. It was dated April 12, ten days before the Squire's death.

'She is here still. It is a new life which I lead while she is near me. Nothing can come of it but sorrow and parting; yet the lightest sound of her footstep thrills me with joy, an accidental touch from her little hand sets all my pulses throbbing. I cannot be unhappy in her presence—yet despair sweeps over my soul ever and anon, like a cloud across a sunlit landscape. My loved one, my dearest! why did we not meet sooner, or why meet at all? Two lives are sacrificed to a caprice of destiny—a cruel, hard, and inexplicable fatality, which rolls on like an iron wheel, and grinds men's hearts into the dust. I am almost an unbeliever when I think how Nature meant my sweet love for me, and me for her, and how Fate has come between and sundered us!'

'Poor Naomi! How true and good she is! How noble, single-minded, frank, unsuspecting. There shall be no more reviling of destiny. I will struggle with this wicked passion—struggle and conquer—or if I fail, end all!'

'Or if I fail, end all,' Arnold repeated musingly.

'Yes, my Naomi, I will remember the days when you were all the world to me—when I had no sweeter hope than a placid life spent in your company, when that calm friendship and reverent admiration which I felt for you seemed to me all that is best and noblest in love. For the sake of those days I will conquer myself and be true to you; and if there can be no more happiness for me, there shall at least be peace and quiet days and a conscience at ease. Perhaps, after all, those things constitute real happiness, and this fever-dream of passion is but a mock beatitude, like the wild brief joys of delirium, the flashes of unreasoning delight that fire the maniac's brain for a moment, to leave him lost in deepest gloom. O no, I do *not* believe that passion means happiness, any more than storm and lightning mean fine weather. Both are grand, both are beautiful; and they leave ruin and death behind them.'

'When honour ceases to be my guide, let me perish.'

'Death hovers near us, and our thoughts are full of sadness. A few days, a few hours may bring the inevitable end. Where she is, there is always sunshine. Her presence soothes me like tenderest music—like the songs my mother sang beside my cradle!

'God help me, for my heart is breaking!'

Arnold read on for an hour. The journal continued in the same strain, with much repetition of motive—going over the same ground very often, as the writer argued with himself, and made good resolves, which were evidently broken as soon as made. It was the old story of a fatal unconquerable passion. Sometimes the sorrow deepened to despair, and Arnold read with a sinking of the heart, feeling that a man who could write thus might not be very far from the suicide's state of mind.

The name of the object of such an unhappy love was not once written, and there was a general vagueness in the journal which left Arnold considerably in the dark. He only knew that the woman his brother loved had been one who lived near him— with whom he was almost daily associated—some one belonging to Combhaven. Who could she be? Arnold was very sure that he had never seen the original of those delicate pencillings in his brother's book. Oswald's likenesses of Naomi were good enough to prove that there must be some degree of likeness in the other portraits—unless, indeed, these were not portraits, only the semblance of some airy nothing that lived but in the draftsman's fancy.

No, the same face appeared too often not to be real. The face and the confession of a fatal love came too near each other in the book for Arnold to doubt that the sketches were faithful portraits.

'I have been to the parish church every Sunday since I came home, and I have seen no face that bears the faintest resemblance to this,' thought Arnold, sorely perplexed.

Naomi could perchance have enlightened him. Naomi must have known to whom her lover's heart had gone forth when she lost him; but it would have been direst cruelty to ask Naomi such a question.

'And if I knew all, would it tell me my brother's fate?' Arnold wondered sorrowfully; for since he had seen Oswald's diary it seemed to him that self-destruction was no improbable end for the writer.

'When a man once gets out of the right line, who can tell how far he may stray?' thought the sailor.

CHAPTER IX.

REPUDIATED.

Captain Pentreath went back to London on business of his own. He had to wind up his affairs with the shipowners who had employed him from the beginning of his career; and this was no easy matter, for the owners had rarely had so good a captain, and were disinclined to lose him. Arnold had made up his mind that his place was on shore for some time to come. His brother had left him the stewardship of his estate, and he meant to be faithful to that trust till Oswald came back to claim his own, if it pleased God to bring him safely back by and by—a result for which Arnold most fervently prayed. The neglect into which all things had fallen appealed strongly to the Captain's love of order; there was a pleasure for him in making crooked things straight. He assumed the command at Combhaven with as much decision as if he had been on board ship; and people obeyed him as well as his sailors had done; and it is to be remarked that the most popular commander is the captain who is best obeyed.

Business kept him in London some time; but when he went back to Combhaven he was a free man, and his career as land steward lay before him —till Oswald's return. Hope had argued the question with fear, until Arnold had taught himself to believe that the idea of Oswald's suicide was a morbid delusion of Joshua Haggard's, and that, sooner or later, the welcome letter would come, from some remote spot of earth, to say that the young Squire had forgotten his griefs, and was happy, and homeward bound.

It was May when Captain Pentreath returned to the Grange in this more hopeful state of mind. The Exeter coach came in to Combhaven at five o'clock in the afternoon, and after a hasty dinner Arnold went straight to the minister's house. He had made no friendships in his native place, and it seemed to him that Naomi Haggard was the nearest and dearest to him in his home. Had Oswald remained true, she would have been his sister. He felt all a brother's tenderness for her already.

'She shall be my sister,' he told himself; 'my friend and counsellor. Both our lives have been made lonely.'

Mr. Haggard's family had just finished tea when Arnold was ushered into the parlour. Sally had been carrying out the tea-board when she heard his knock, and had been so flurried by such an unusual circumstance as to be scarcely able to deposit her burden on the kitchen-table without loss or damage. When she opened the door and saw Captain Pentreath, she gave utterance to one of those suppressed screams with which she always greeted his likeness to his brother. 'It was like seeing the young Squire come back again, broader chested and nobler looking,' she told Jim, with whom she was on more confidential terms than with any other member of the household. Aunt Judith had gone back to the shop; Naomi sat reading by the open window; Joshua was in his armchair, his head thrown back upon the cushion, his eyes half closed, resting after one of those pilgrimages over hill and dale which had of late sorely exhausted him. His whole life was much more exhausting than it had been, the candle was being burned more fiercely. Traces of fatigue showed plainly in the sharpened lines of his face, in the pallor of his skin, and the shadows about his eyes.

There was no one else in the room.

Joshua Haggard opened his eyes and started up. He looked at Arnold curiously for a moment or so, as if he scarcely knew him—like a man not quite released from the thraldom of a dream.

'I am afraid I've disturbed you in a comfortable nap, Mr. Haggard,' said Arnold.

'No, I was hardly asleep—only resting.'

'You look as if you had much need of rest.'

'Do I?' asked the minister musingly. 'Well, the scabbard must wear out in time, I suppose. It matters little, if the sword is only bright till the last.'

'You don't ask me if I have found out anything about my brother in London,' said Arnold.

'Because I don't expect to hear that you have. I have told you my opinion,' replied Joshua gloomily.

'It is an opinion which I will never entertain until it is forced upon me by positive proof. My watchword is hope—yes, Naomi, hope,' he added, turning to Joshua's daughter, who was looking at him gravely, with no answering ray of hope in her sad eyes.

He held out his hand to her, and they shook hands warmly, like brother and sister. Joshua sank back into his chair, and took up an open volume from the table, and resumed his reading, as if to indicate that he had no more to say to his visitor.

This reception was so cold as to be scarcely civil; but Arnold was not going to take offence easily. He wanted to know more of Naomi. In his mind she was the only person who could thoroughly sympathise with him in his longing for the absent, or in his grief for the lost. She alone in Combhaven had fondly loved his brother.

He began to talk of indifferent subjects, trying to infuse a little cheerfulness into the conversation; but there was a leaden gloom in the atmosphere of the minister's parlour which Arnold had no power to brighten. Naomi listened and replied with grave attention.

She was gentle and friendly, but he could not win a smile from her. She seemed weighed down by an unconquerable melancholy.

'Do they ever smile, I wonder?' thought Arnold. 'Or has the household always this funereal air? Is it grief for my absent brother that makes her so sad? I should have given her credit for strength of mind to surmount such a grief, or at least to hide it. And the parson—well, I suppose that gloomy cast of countenance is simply professional.'

Despite Naomi's lack of cheerfulness, Captain Pentreath was interested in her. That melancholy look lent a poetic air to her beauty. He felt that she was a woman of deepest feelings, one who would love but once and love for ever. Even Oswald's inconstancy had not weakened her affection. He would have given much to be alone with her again for a little while, to have talked freely with her, heart to heart. He felt as if he could have spoken about his brother, and his brother's errors, without wounding her. But that figure of the minister sitting between him and the light oppressed him like a waking nightmare. There came an awkward silence presently, and Arnold felt he had no more to say, and must needs take his leave.

He had just risen to depart when the door opened, and a girl with fair hair, pale face, and Puritan cap, came into the room.

At sight of him she gave a faint cry and put her hand to her heart, and then, with a great effort of self-restraint, made him a grave curtsy, and crossed the room to an empty chair near Joshua.

'My God!' cried Arnold, turning very pale.

The sudden apparition wrung the exclamation from him before he had time to summon up his self-command. This was the face he had seen in his brother's journal. This was Joshua's young wife, of whose girlish beauty he had heard people talk, but whom he had never seen till this moment, for she had been ailing of late, and had kept much in her own room. And this was Oswald's fatal love—a love so wildly foolish, so deeply dishonourable, that it might well work the ruin of him who harboured it.

Joshua looked up as the door opened, and heard Cynthia's cry and Arnold's ejaculation, and saw the pale startled look of the one, the utter amazement of the other.

'He will be like his brother, perhaps,' he thought gloomily, and an angry shadow stole over his dark face. He looked at his wife as she seated herself quietly near him. She was very white and her lips trembled. This sudden appearance of Oswald Pentreath's brother affected her as if she had seen a ghost.

Arnold took a hurried leave of the minister and his daughter, made a grave bow to Cynthia, and was gone. He could not have conversed calmly after the revelation which had surprised and shocked him. It was an awful thing to know that his brother had been guilty enough to fix his affections here.

Did Joshua know or suspect the truth? Yes, Arnold thought, he did suspect, and this suspicion was the cause of his coldness about Oswald, and that gloomy tone which suggested animosity.

Having discovered the fatal siren who had beguiled his brother from the paths of peace, Arnold's next desire was to be able to question her about his brother's fate. Who so likely to be in the secret of Oswald's intentions at the time he left Combhaven as the woman he loved? Doubtless he had contrived to see her during his last brief residence at the Grange, and he had told her what he meant to do with his life.

The difficulty was for Arnold to obtain an interview with Joshua's wife without doing harm of some kind. Joshua was unfriendly and repellent in his manner, very ready to suspect evil, no doubt, of any one bearing the name of Pentreath. Arnold had also to consider Naomi's feelings. It was just possible that she was ignorant of her stepmother's part in the tragedy of her life.

Accident brought about a meeting which could have been only contrived with difficulty. Arnold had been out for a long rambling ride on Herne on the third day after his return to the Grange, and coming slowly homeward in the afternoon sunlight, he overtook Cynthia Haggard walking alone in one of the green lanes just outside Combhaven. She was walking very slowly, with bent head and listless step, like one whose thoughts are far away from the scenes that surround her.

The full western sunlight shone through the young oak leaves, the hawthorns were fleecy masses of white blossom, and filled the air with perfume, the sea glittered above the waving line of the hedge, and through the deep cleft in the rich red bank the little town of Combhaven showed its tiled roofs and many gables, its mellow thatches and cool gray slates, and shining ochre walls that seemed made of sunlight.

Arnold slipped quietly from his horse and put the bridle over his arm. Herne, having been as fiendish in behaviour as in name during the first half of his day's work, was now in a calm and philosophic mood, and cropped the young ferns contently.

'Mrs. Haggard, may I have a few words with you?' Arnold asked gently.

Cynthia had looked up startled at the sound of the horse's hoofs. She dropped a curtsy, and answered nervously,

'If you please, sir.'

'You wonder what I can have to say to you, perhaps?'

'Yes, sir.'

'And yet you must know that my mind is full of anxiety about my brother.'

Her cheek crimsoned, and then paled.

'I am—we are all anxious,' she said. 'It is so strange that he has not written to you. He was not likely to write to any one else—but to you, his brother, of whom he was so fond.'

'You have heard him talk about me, then?' inquired Arnold.

'Very often. He looked forward so anxiously to your return.'

'Would to God I had come sooner! I might have kept him at home, perhaps. Come, Mrs. Haggard, be candid with me. This mystery about my brother is making me very wretched. Cannot you help me? You may know something, perhaps, which no one else knows—something which might enlighten me as to his intentions when he left home. For Heaven's sake, be truthful with me. Do not be afraid to trust me. I know the trouble that made my brother leave his country. A diary of his fell into my hands a little while ago, with the story of his unhappy love written in it. I know that it was for your sake he became an exile. I implore you to tell me all you can that may help me to discover his fate.'

Cynthia trembled, and grew deadly pale, yet looked at her questioner steadily. There was innocence in the look, Arnold thought. This was no guilty wife—but, not the less, a most unhappy woman.

'I know that he was going to America,' answered Cynthia, 'and I know no more than that.'

'Did you see him on that last day?'

'I did. Pray do not tell Naomi or any one else. No one knows of our meeting. It was a secret. He wished to say good-bye to me before he went.'

'Were you the last person who saw him?'

'I think so. When he left me he was going to the coach.'

'Are you sure he meant to go by the coach?'

'He told me so.'

Arnold's countenance fell. This gave a darker aspect to the affair.

'What time in the day did you see him?'

'About four o'clock in the afternoon.'

'And where did you meet?

'Will you promise to tell no one?'

'Yes, I promise.'

'On Matcherly Common, by the old shaft.'

'I know the place. We have played there many a time when we were children. Are you sure that no one knew of your meeting?'

'Quite sure.'

'And that no one met you, or watched you, that afternoon?'

'I saw no one. I do not believe that any one saw me.'

'My brother told you he meant to leave by the coach; yet he did not leave by it. You saw him at four o'clock that last afternoon, and I cannot hear of any one who saw him after that hour. It is strange—alarming even—is it not?'

'Very strange. But I trust in God that he is safe; though we do not know where he is.'

'That's an easy way of putting it,' said Arnold, with a shade of bitterness.

'No one can be more sorry for him than I am,'

answered Cynthia, with a sudden sob. 'It is my sin to be so sorry.'

'Poor child! Forgive me for speaking harshly. I fancy sometimes that every one except myself is indifferent to my brother's fate. Your husband thinks he committed suicide; but I can't and won't believe that. You don't believe it, do you?' he asked, turning upon her quickly.'

'O, no, no, no!' she cried, with a startled look of pain, as if the idea were new to her. 'He would never do that. He would never be so wild—so guilty—as to shoot himself, like Werther.'

'Who is Werther?'

'A man in a book your brother read to us; but it was a real person, who was very unhappy, and who shot himself. He did not seem to know that suicide was a sin. But I cannot believe that Oswald would be so rash. O, no, no, God forbid that he should be tempted to such a dreadful deed! I cannot think it. He was very calm when we bade each other good-bye. He blessed me, and promised to take more heed of serious things in days to come than he had done in days past.'

'And there was no wildness in his manner? He did not talk like a desperate man?'

'No, indeed.'

'I thank you for having been truthful and frank. It is a sad story. Would to God that he had been constant and faithful to that noble girl, your stepdaughter!'

He could not spare her this implied reproach. His brother's fate seemed ever so much darker to him after what he had just heard. And for all this sorrow and uncertainty, the fair young creature standing by his side was in some measure to blame. Even that last secret meeting might have been in some wise the turning-point of his destiny.

'Had you been in the habit of meeting my brother secretly?' he asked presently. 'Had you met him often before that day?'

'Never in my life before,' answered Cynthia, with an indignant look; 'I should not have gone then, even though he made my going a last favour, if I had not had a purpose in seeing him. I thought I might win him back to Naomi. I knew he had once loved her dearly; and I thought perhaps it needed but a few words to awaken the old love in his heart.'

'And do you think you were the best preacher to preach that sermon?' asked Arnold. 'Well, you acted for the best, I daresay; and again I thank you for your candour. But I am no nearer the secret of my brother's fate than I was an hour ago. Good-bye!'

He raised his hat and left her with a somewhat formal salutation, not offering her his hand. There was resentment in his heart against this fair-faced wife who had spoiled Naomi's life and his own. He led Herne to the end of the lane, and there mounted him, and trotted quickly home, the sagacious animal scenting the oats and clover in his now luxurious stable.

Cynthia walked slowly on, crying a little in a languid helpless way, like one who was accustomed to solitude and tears. The sharp sound of Herne's hoofs died away in the distance. A lark was singing loud and shrill in the high blue sky, and there was a drowsy bee among the hawthorns, but all the rest of Nature was silent. Suddenly there broke upon that summer stillness a loud rustling of boughs, and a man sprang through a gap in the hedge and confronted her.

She looked up, full of sudden fear, expecting to see some unknown ruffian bent on robbery or murder; but the dark and angry face looking into hers was the face of her husband.

'Joshua! How you frightened me!'

'No doubt. Women who meet their lovers in secret are easily startled.'

'My lover! Joshua, are you mad? I have been talking to Captain Pentreath, who overtook me by chance a little while ago.'

'By chance! Do you think I am going to believe that story? Woman, I know you too well. Satan set you in my path for my undoing—to the peril and loss of my soul; for my ruin and destruction here and hereafter. Fool, fool, fool!'—this with a cry of anguish, striking his forehead with his clenched fists—'I ought to have known it was a snare—the fair strange face under the burning summer sky; the gipsy waif, homeless, nameless, a stranger to Christ and salvation! Spawn of Beelzebub, why did I not recognise you?'

'Joshua, for pity's sake! I am your true wife; I have honoured and obeyed you—'

'Honoured! Was it to honour me you lured that young man to his doom? Was it for my honour you met him and kissed him? Yes; I saw him holding you in his arms under God's all-seeing eye; clasping you to his breast, as I held you that accursed night when I thought myself the happiest among men, because I had won you for my own. Won you! O thou incarnate falsehood! fair as an angel to the eye, foul as sin to the heart that knows thee! And having tempted one brother to death and doom eternal, you are spreading your nets for the other. You would have him, too. You are like her that waiteth at the street-corner, "in the twilight, in the evening, in the black and dark night. Her house is the way to hell, going down to the chambers of death. Yea, verily, her feet go down to death; her steps take hold on hell." Away with you, fair devil!'

His arm was raised to strike; but she fell on

her knees, and thus by a happy chance escaped the degrading blow, and saved her husband that last shame.

'Joshua, what madness has seized you? I never wronged you willingly, as God knows. If I did do you wrong, it is because human nature is weak, and God does not always stand by us. He lets us stand alone a little while in order to show us how weak we are without Him, how soon we stumble and fall when that heavenly hand is withdrawn. Yes, husband, I have been a sinner. God hid His face for a time. Oswald loved me, and I loved him, and forgot my wickedness in the sweetness of being beloved by him. It was like a dream. But when he spoke of his love my heart awakened, and I was your true wife. I have said no word to him—never, from first to last—that I dare not repeat to you, or that I am ashamed to remember. I am your true wife, and honour and revere you now as I did that first day when you took me to the only decent home I had ever known. Have I forgotten what I owe you, Joshua? O no, no, no! I am not so base, nor so ungrateful.'

'Your speech is like your face,' said Joshua, with set teeth—'passing fair, passing fair. But I know you, pretty one! Yes; look up, eyes, blue as God's summer sky—look up in sad innocent wonder! A lie, a lie, nothing but a lie! Satan has made you so: he painted your cheeks, and limned your smile and every delicate feature, that you might lure good men to death and hell. Can he work without his instruments, do you think? He does not walk this earth in palpable shape, lest we should know him and avoid him; but he puts on such a pretty garb as yours, and counts his worshippers by the score. Every priestess such as you brings a crowd to his altar. But I have done with you. I have rent the net; I will have no further dealings with you; I will see your false face no more!'

'Joshua, have pity!'

'"Can a man take fire in his bosom and not be burned?"'

'Joshua!'

'"He that doeth it destroyeth his own soul. A wound and dishonour shall he get; and his reproach shall not be wiped away."'

'Joshua, can you believe that there was any harm, any wrong against you, in my meeting with Captain Pentreath just now?' cried Cynthia, still at her husband's feet, looking up at him in an agony of supplication, trying to grasp those strong cruel hands that thrust her from him.

'I know that you are false to the core. I know that Satan made you to lead me down to the pit. What do I know about you and Captain Pentreath? Very little. I was just in time for the fag-end of your interview. I came across the field, and saw you through a break in the hedge. You were standing in close converse with him, just as you were with his brother—'

'Ah,' cried Cynthia, startled, 'you were there that day—you saw us. You said so just now.'

'The kisses were over, I daresay,' continued Joshua, too much beside himself to heed this interruption. 'The kisses were done with before I came. He heard my step, perhaps, and so left you with a formal salutation, as if you were strangers parting. Hypocrites, liars both—children of the accursed! But I have done with you. I turn my face away from Satan and his witchcraft, and I will make my peace with God before I die. Go back—go back to your tents, to the children of Baal! Go back to your juggleries and mummeries, and leave me to repent of my folly—to put on sackcloth and ashes—to go up alone among the hills, like Elijah in the mountains, to wait for the advent of my God!'

'Joshua, for mercy's sake be calm; speak to me quietly, that I may know what you really mean. I have no wish but to obey you. If you say that I am to go away from you—to go back and be a servant, and work for my daily bread as I did before I was your wife—I shall go, and make no complaint. But I am your true and obedient wife all the same. Do not doubt that. I will obey you when you are cruel, just as I obeyed you when you were kind, and I shall never murmur.'

'Fair of speech, and fair of face,' muttered Joshua. 'Yes, Lucifer, her master, was beautiful as the morning star.'

'Do you mean to turn me out of doors, Joshua? Do you mean that your home is to be mine no longer?'

'I do. You have brought misery and shame into my house. You have poisoned my cup, turned my daily bread to ashes. I would fain be rid of you for ever. I cannot serve God while you are near me. Satan is too strong for me while he works under such a mask.'

'And you wish us to part,' she said deliberately, 'for ever?'

'Yes; I love my imperishable soul better than that viler human heart which cleaves to you. In heaven there is neither marrying nor giving in marriage. In heaven I shall forget the anguish of an unsatisfied love.'

'Joshua, I am your servant, to obey you in this as in all things. You have but to say you wish me gone, and I shall go. When you cease to pity, God will forgive and take pity on me, because He does not make our burdens too heavy for us. Do you remember that night in the pine-wood, Joshua, when you took me to your heart and told me that I was precious in your sight? I said then that I was not good enough to be your wife; that it would be happiness for me to be your servant, and wait upon you and work for you, and gather words of wisdom from your lips. But you would have it otherwise. I was wiser in this, you see; for now you are weary of me, and want to send me away. Let it be so, then; I will forget that I am your wife, and remember only that I am your servant, and bound to obey in all things. I am your servant, and you have dismissed me. I can go back to Penmoyle and work for my living—far away, where I shall not disgrace you. Good-bye, sir.'

She took his hand and kissed it, still on her knees. He shuddered at the contact of those rose-bud lips, but never looked at her. His eyes were fixed on the distant sea-line—wide-open eyes gazing blankly at the blue bright light.

'Am I really to go, Joshua?' Cynthia asked meekly, after a brief silence, in which the hum of insects, the sharp whirring sound of the grasshopper, filled the air.

He passed his hand across his brow wearily.

'Get thee behind me, Satan. Yes, go, go, go! I can never scale the walls of God's eternal city while this weight of earthly passion cleaves to me. Go far out of my reach, lest I should slay you; and think of your dead lover, and repent your sin.'

'What! he *is* dead, then—and you know it?' she exclaimed, with a bitter cry.

'Yes,' answered Joshua, flinging her away from him into the dust; 'go and weep and howl for him. It was your sin that slew him!'

She lay for a little while where he had thrown her, on the sun-baked grass of the bank, amongst the ferns and wild flowers—not quite unconscious, but with a brain in which strange and familiar images whirled wildly as in a demon dance. Then came a few moments in which all was blank—moments of blessed repose; and then she staggered to her feet, and looked round her. The lane was empty. Joshua had said his last word, and was gone.

She stood looking round her in the westering sunshine, pondering what she ought to do. Not for an instant did she contemplate rebellion against her husband's decree. He had bidden her to leave him, and she would go away, meekly, uncomplainingly, as Hagar went out into the wilderness.

'Ah me,' she said to herself piteously, comparing herself with Hagar, 'I have no Ishmael to be my comfort and hope.'

It never occurred to her to go back to her husband's house, and claim the place which was hers by right, and which no act of hers had forfeited. She did not even contemplate going back to claim her own—the clothes and books and small possessions dear to womanhood which she had acquired since her marriage. Empty-handed and penniless as when Joshua found her sitting by the water-pool on the distant Cornish waste, she left the scene of her brief and hapless married life. She had neither purse nor scrip—not so much as a few shillings to help her on her way. But she turned her pale face steadily to the west, and set out to walk to Penmoyle. In all this wide world she had no other friends than the spinster sisters whom she could turn to for a refuge in her desolation, and even from them she could not feel quite sure of a kind reception. They had offered her their friendship, telling her on the day she left them to appeal to them in any hour of need. But how would they receive her when she told them that

Joshua had cast her off—they who reverenced Joshua as a saint and prophet?

To them she must needs turn in her distress, having no other earthly haven. She had served them faithfully in the past, and had won their favour; and she was willing to serve them in the future for her daily bread, and nightly shelter, and the privilege of worshipping her God in the faith Joshua had taught her. She thought of the white-haired old minister, with his gentle old-world manners and his ready kindness. She remembered how his praise had thrilled her at the thought that Joshua would hear of her well-doing and be glad. And now all was over. Joshua hated her; Joshua spurned her as a vile and guilty creature. No man's praise, no woman's favour, could ever lift her up in his esteem any more. She was degraded and cast off for ever.

Well, she could be a servant again, and toil for her bread and serve her God in patience so long as life's burden was laid upon her. It seemed to her that the road along which she had to carry her burden was not interminable. A little way off there came a region of mist and cloud, entering which she would be at peace, and would lay down her load, and rest her weary head upon the sweetest pillow, and let her tired eyelids close amidst a divine sunshine, a light as of the resurrection morning, when the glad sunbeams danced upon the hill-tops.

It was a long way from Combhaven to that little village high up among the rolling Cornish tors. Cynthia could not calculate the number of miles; but she had an idea that Penmoyle was very far away—many days' journey at the rate at which she could walk, which was slow, for her cough and low fever had left her weak.

'Luckily I know how to sleep under a haystack, and I am not ashamed to beg my bread when I see a kind face at a cottage-door,' she said to herself.

She had her silver watch and chain, which she thought she might sell in one of the towns she had to pass through; and there was the gold keeper above her wedding-ring—this too she might dispose of, if hard pressed by want; but if people were kind she could get on without money, so little would serve to keep body and soul together.

So she set out on her journey, a new Hagar, but with no sweet child companion to make the desert blossom like the rose.

CHAPTER X.

WHAT THE COWBOY COULD TELL.

AFTER his interview with Cynthia Haggard, Captain Pentreath reasoned himself into an easier state of mind about his missing brother. His sanguine nature leaned towards the brighter view of the question. Oswald had been calm and resigned when he parted with the object of his fatal love; he had gone away to begin a new life, had cast off the fetters of passion, and gone forth a free man.

'I shall hear from him in due time. All will be well,' said Arnold.

Having made up his mind deliberately to go on hoping, and, indeed, entertaining the conviction that the riddle of his brother's destiny would be solved in time, Arnold Pentreath considered it his duty to inspire Naomi with the same hopeful view. It afflicted him to see her pale sad face, to watch her slow listless movements. It became his most ardent desire to cheer and console her.

With this end he went very often to the minister's house, and sat in the quiet old parlour where Oswald had spent so many hours of his life, and talked to Naomi while she sewed. There was no one to object to his visits. Aunt Judith was in the shop; Joshua was away, no one knew whither. It was his habit now to come home wearied at nightfall, save on those evenings when he had class-meetings, or Bible-meetings, or some kind of service in his chapel.

Cynthia was gone, and Joshua had accounted briefly for her absence by stating that she had gone to see her friends at Penmoyle.

'You had better send her trunk on by the coach,' said Joshua to Naomi.

'But why did she go so suddenly, father?' Naomi asked, puzzled by this disruption of the household.

'Because it was her whim to go, and it was not my pleasure to say her nay.'

'Has she gone by the coach?'

'I suppose so.'

'And when is she to come back?'

'When I please to bid her come.'

Naomi sighed, and obeyed her father's order. Alas for this change, which made her father a person to be obeyed with fear and trembling rather than with faith and love! Naomi had not forgiven Cynthia for all the misery she had wrought; but this sudden disappearance of her father's wife oppressed her with a sense of injustice and wrong done by Joshua. With what cruelty had he driven that meek and sorrowful offender away from him? His daughter had noted his conduct to his wife, and had seen his harshness, his coldness, his growing aversion—the chilling mask which passionate love puts on when jealousy gnaws the heart.

Cynthia was gone, and Naomi's life was now quite lonely. She was glad of Arnold's visit, and took some comfort from his hopeful talk about the absent master of the Grange.

'He will come back to his home and to you, Naomi,' said the Captain. 'Come back a new man, and an honest one, proud to redeem his faith.'

'Were he to come back to-morrow I should give him a sister's loving welcome,' answered Naomi, 'but never more than a sister's love. He has broken my heart once—I won't let him break it again.'

'But if he were honestly repentant and sincere, Naomi?'

'He might believe himself sincere. I could not trust him with my peace. Do not think that I am angry with him. I am only sorry that he should ever have been so mistaken as to believe in the reality of his love for me. He never knew what love meant till he gave his heart where it should not have been given.'

'Well, Naomi, perhaps you are wise. The vessel that fails to answer to her helm in the hour of danger is hardly a ship to be trusted. Then we will think of Oswald as an absent brother only, and look forward hopefully to his return.'

'God knows I try to hope for it,' said Naomi, with a sigh.

'Why should he not be really your brother—brother in fact as well as in name?' pleaded Arnold, taking her unresisting hands. 'Make him your brother, Naomi, by making me your husband. We have not known each other very long, but our mutual sorrow has brought us nearer together than years of common acquaintance could have done. I have looked into your heart, Naomi, and I know its worth. Let me take my brother's place, dear; I shall never wander; my love shall know no change. It is founded on a rock—for it was my esteem for your noble nature which first taught me to love you.'

Naomi withdrew her hands from his, and stood up, looking at him seriously, with eyes full of tears.

'Never again let this be spoken of between us, Arnold,' she said. 'It can never be.'

'Why not?'

'There is a reason which you must never know.'

'But I am not to be satisfied like that, Naomi. There is no reason that I can recognise, unless you say that you do not love me—can never teach yourself to love me.'

'I will say that, then—I can never love you.'

'And your eyes are brimming with tears, and your lips tremble as you say the words. It is not true, Naomi; it is a lie—a lie against the might of love. You love me as I love you, and we were meant for each other and for happiness. Why should you or I be miserable all our lives because a foolish young man has run away from felicity? Naomi, dearest love, make my life happy.'

'You are good, and I honour you; you are like Oswald, and my heart yearns towards you,' answered the girl falteringly, for it seemed to her at this moment as if the picture of a new life were suddenly unfolded before her eyes, and the vision was marvellously bright; 'but I can never be more than your friend and sister.'

'I see. You love the truant still. Did I not say so?'

'His memory is very dear to me.'

Arnold said no more. Those eloquent eyes, those tremulous lips, had told him he was beloved, and yet this love was denied him. What was he to think? He was hardly inclined to despair, or to accept this answer of Naomi's as final. She had some mistaken notion of fidelity to a departed love

doubtless; she would sacrifice a lover in the present
—a real and living affection—for the sake of that
inconstant lover in the past.

'Patience,' thought Arnold; 'I shall be able to
talk her out of her folly sooner or later.'

Meanwhile he was content to be accepted on the
friendly and brotherly footing. He contrived to see
Naomi very often. He found his way even into the
wilderness, that burial-ground of dead joys and bitter
memories. He met her in all her walks. It was
difficult for her not to think that her lost lover had
come back to her with a nobler mind and larger
ideas. Here she found no languid indolence, no
placid unconcern for the welfare of others, so long
as summer skies were blue, and one could lie at ease
under the beeches reading Byron. Arnold was full
of care for the labourers on his patrimonial estate,
full of sympathy and kindness for the struggling
tenant farmers and their industrious wives, for the
young men who desired a little more enlightenment
and education than their fathers had deemed need-
ful for the fulness of life's measure. With Arnold
benevolent deeds were not castles in the air, Utopian

schemes to be set on foot in some convenient hour of the future, but duties to be done at once, now, while it was yet day.

Arnold was glad of so intelligent a sympathiser with his cares as steward of his brother's fortune. Naomi was always ready to help him with counsel and experience. She had visited among the labouring poor, and knew their needs and shortcomings—knew where disease found them weakest, how fever crept into their dwellings.

'I can't think what I should do without you,' said Arnold; and it was a new happiness to Naomi to feel that she had been useful. Life at home was so empty and barren, her duties mechanically performed, her service unrecognised. The change in her father had made the very atmosphere of home gloomy and oppressive.

Cynthia had been away nearly a month, and there had been no tidings of her. This seemed strange to all the household, but as Joshua expressed neither wonder nor anxiety, it was supposed that his wife's absence was understood and approved by him.

'Poor weak-minded mortal,' sighed aunt Judith, after discussing the question with her niece at their lonely tea-table; 'the first time I saw that pink and white piece of prettiness step across the threshold I knew what he was laying up for himself. A man of his years can't set his heart upon a wax doll without paying the penalty; above all when it's a doll that has neither parents, nor a good stock of house-linen, nor decent bringing up. *I* knew what was coming,' cried aunt Judith, with a laugh of exultant irony, 'and my only wonder is that things haven't turned out much worse.'

'Poor thing!' sighed Naomi, thinking with some touch of compunction of the pale sad face from which she had averted her eyes so coldly of late. 'Do you think father sent her away?'

'If he did he'd have done no more than was right,' said aunt Judith. 'And if he'd done it when I first tried to open his eyes about her he'd have shown himself a wiser man. But whether she got tired of her life here and went off of her own free will, or whether your father sent her, matters very little to us. She's gone,' concluded the spinster decisively, 'and I hope it's not unchristianlike to wish she may never come back.'

Having put the idea of his brother's suicide out of his mind, Arnold had not attached any dark meaning to his interview with Cynthia. Her statement seemed to him natural and credible, and rather calculated to reassure than to alarm. Oswald had been calm and resigned. He had stated his intention of going to a new world, to begin a new life. What ground was there for supposing that a man in this frame of mind had been so false to manhood as to take his own life? Arnold sent to an Exeter bookseller for the *Sorrows of Werther*, and read the story carefully; but not being of so sentimental a turn as his brother, and not being in love with another man's wife, he had found the reading rather a laborious business, and Werther a weak-minded youth with a fatal habit of prosing about his own emotions.

'God forbid that my brother should ever follow the example of such a booby!' said Arnold, when he had seen Werther laid in his unconsecrated grave, in the memorable blue coat and yellow waistcoat, with Charlotte's pink breast-knot in his pocket; 'I should have as much contempt for his want of sense as regret for his want of religion.'

Arnold had not yet gone to look at the spot where Oswald had parted from Mrs. Haggard. He remembered the scene well enough in days gone by; the lonely common with its hillocks and hollows and marshy spots, over which the swift-winged plover skimmed lightly, vanishing with a shrill cry into blue distance. The scene was so familiar to him that it had no special significance; it never struck him that just that one spot of all others, that little bit of sunburnt common by the abandoned mine, might be fatal—that here yawned a natural grave, ready for the end of a tragedy.

He went up to an old farmhouse one afternoon, to settle a question of roofing and thatching which had been for some time in discussion. It was the last house on the way to Matcherly Common, a house that stood on the edge of the wood, or almost in the wood. The latticed casements looked down a beechen glade. It was a place of silence and soft cool shadows, a welcome retreat on a summer's day like this on which Arnold rode over to settle matters with Farmer Westall about his granary roofs.

Herne had been made happy in a spacious stable where the good old white wagon-horses dozed over their hay and clover, and where the thud of a ponderous tail whisked round for the slaughter of a forest-fly and the slow munching of fodder were the only sounds that broke the slumberous stillness. Captain Pentreath had made his inspection of the premises, and was drinking a glass of Mrs. Westall's famous perry before departing, when the farmer mentioned a subject which always found Arnold an attentive listener.

'You haven't heerd anything of your brother, I suppose, Captain?'

'Not a line. But I don't despair of getting news of him before long. He's not been gone a twelvemonth yet, you see, Mr. Westall, and a year is a short time when a man has to cross the sea. He may have changed his mind about America, and gone to New South Wales, and that's half a year's voyage to begin with.'

'That's where the convicks go, ain't it, Captain? The young Squire 'ud never go theer, surely.'

'There's no knowing how far a man may go when he's once made up his mind to turn rover,' said Arnold cheerily.

'Ah,' sighed the farmer, 'this here world of ours be a strange un; there's things in it that puzzles my poor old wits a'most as much as that theer thatch catchin' fire the identical day arter I refused aunt Nancy the faggit.'

There was a lurking significance in this remark that caught Arnold's attention.

'You have heard something about my brother!' he cried; 'you can tell me something! For God's sake keep nothing from me; it is a matter of life or death.'

'The by's a truth-spoken by,' said the farmer, 'or I shouldn't ha' listened to un.'

'What boy?'

'It isn't because a by earns his bit o' mate minding cows that he hasn't got a soul to be saved,' continued the farmer, as deliberately as if pursuing a philosophical argument; 'and I can't say as ever I ound out this here lad in a lie.'

'Will you tell me what you mean, how this bears upon my brother?' cried Arnold, breathless with impatience.

'My wife and me have sat under Mr. Haggard for the last ten years. He was the first to tell us our souls were in danger o' everlasting fire, and he's gone on warning of us ever since. 'Tain't likely I'm going to speak agen him.'

'Speak plainly at any rate,' exclaimed Arnold, 'if you mean anything. And from your manner it's clear you mean something. What has this boy of yours to do with my brother's fate?'

'It ain't what he has to do, but what he can tell. It was a hot summer day, you may remember, that day as the young Squire were last seen at Combhaven—harvest time, and reg'lar harvest weather. This lad o' mine, Tim, was out in the forest mindin' cows. But perhaps you'd sooner hear it from the lad's own lips?' suggested the farmer.

'I don't care how I hear it, so long as I hear it quickly!'

'Well, I'll call the by; he's close handy, diggin' taties.'

'Let's go to him,' said Arnold, taking up his whip and gloves.

The farmer wished to bring the boy to the parlour, as a mode of proceeding more consistent with the respect due to his landlord, but the Captain was too eager to endure ceremony. He hurried to the straggling old kitchen-garden at the back of the house, where ancient espaliers which had long outgrown their sustaining framework spread wide their arms against the blue June sky.

Here, digging up the smooth golden-skinned potatoes, they found the farmer's cowboy, a frank-looking blue-eyed lad, over whose sunburnt forehead trickled the dew of toil.

'Now look 'ee here, Tim,' said the farmer; 'I want 'ee to tell the Captain what it was you saw and heerd that day in Matcherly Wood, when th' young Squire passed 'ee by.'

The boy wiped his forehead upon his shirt-sleeve, shifted his spade from one hand to the other, and after some moments of obvious embarrassment found a voice.

'I were mindin' cattle in the forest, you see, sir,

and theer were one cow wi' a white face, she were a new un that master had boughten at Barnstaple last market-day, and she were strange, poor thing, and strayed away ever so far up towards the common; and I was goin' arter her, when who should I see but the minister on afore me, goin' right up to the common.'

'Do you mean Mr. Haggard?'

'Surely. And he went on ahead o' me, till he come right out o' the wood, just wheer the old shaft be; and he looked about un a bit, when he got clear o' the trees, and then went into the engine-house. I watched a bit, wonderin' what he were up to; and then I see un standin' just inside the doorway, where there's a lot o' fallen stones and rubbish, and tansy growin' as tall as young trees, and he stood there lookin' out, yet keepin' of hisself hidden like, as if he were watchin' for somebody. And just then I catched sight o' the white-faced cow, ever so far across the common, and I ran arter her.'

'Strange, warn't it?' said the farmer. 'But there's more to tell.'

'I cotched the old cow, and I was takin' of her

back to the wood, when I comes right up agen the young Squire. I was a bit scared at seein' he, for I'd heerd tell as he were away from Combhaven. He didn't take no notice o' me, but went on, swingin' his stick round, and singin' to hisself, soft like. Well, I thowt no more about un, and I was here and theer with they cows, and they would stray up towards the common, though there warn't much but tansy for they to eat up theer; and I were up close to the common about an hour arterwards, when I heerd a shot fired and then another, so close together they might a been one a'most.'

A white blankness spread itself over Arnold's face—the vacant horror of despair. It was some moments before he could speak.

'You ran to see what those shots meant?' he cried.

'I couldn't tell wheer they come from, not for sartain; but I thowt it was somewheer near the old shaft, and I went up theer arter a bit, but theer was nowt to be seen, and no one about. I went into the engine-house, but the minister was gone.'

'Why has this been kept from me?' asked

Arnold. 'Why, in Heaven's name, didn't you let me know this sooner, Westall? You know how anxious I have been about my brother.'

'I only heerd of it t'other day, when I overheerd Timothy talkin' to our Prudence, the dairymaid. He was tellin' her about the shot.'

'Don't you think it was your duty to have told your master, boy?' asked Arnold.

'I didn't think it was any harm. It might ha' been some one firin' at a rabbit or a gull. There's plenty o' say-gulls flies across Matcherly Common.'

'You saw no more—you heard no more?'

'No, there was nowt arter that. It were milkin' time, and I had to take the cows home.'

'Now look here, Westall,' said Captain Pentreath, taking the farmer aside. 'Those shots may mean nothing, or they may mean a great deal. I know my brother was up yonder, by the old shaft, that August day. I know he had an enemy, and was watched and followed. I have no evidence that he was ever seen alive after that day. Till to-day I've hugged myself with the hope that he is living in some distant country, and that I shall hear of him in due time. I begin to think that hope is a delusion, and that he never left this neighbourhood. If he has been murdered, it is my business to bring his murderer to the gallows. But I must first find his murdered body. Will you help me? You've plenty of farm-labourers in your service. Will you help me to search Matcherly Common, and the mine below it?'

CHAPTER XI.

AT HIS DOOR.

Naomi thought long and deeply of that last interview with Arnold Pentreath. She was in nowise inclined to admit to herself that the sea-captain could now, or in any time to come, take the place of his missing brother—that the heart which had been so freely and so entirely given to Oswald could ever belong to another. Yet, while looking upon this change of feeling as impossible, Naomi was conscious that Arnold had begun to exercise a powerful influence upon her mind, and that his most unexpected avowal of affection for her had moved her deeply.

He was like his brother and he loved his brother. These two circumstances were alone sufficient to insure her regard. And now he had paid her the highest tribute that man can offer to woman. He had given her his loyal and kindly heart—that heart whose wide benevolence she had seen in many an unconsidered act of his life; he had tendered her his happiness, his future; and she had found only one cold answer to his prayer: 'It cannot be.'

'If I loved him better than I ever loved Oswald my answer must have been the same,' she said to herself in those long hours of sorrowful meditation which made up the larger half of her joyless life. 'While the dark cloud rests upon Oswald's fate I can have but one answer for any lover—you, Arnold, of all others. How do I know that I have the right to stand up with unbowed head, among honest men and women, when my heart is tortured by the thought that my father—he who preaches the Gospel and exhorts other men to repentance—may be the vilest sinner of all?'

This was the gist of Naomi's meditations. She had tried to put that awful fear away from her, but it was rooted in her heart. As weeks and months went by and brought no news of Oswald, the fear grew stronger; and with the fear came remorse, a slow and consuming anguish. Had she been but patient, had she borne her own burden in silence and kept the secret of that cruel letter, this horror need never have been. She had put the scorpion into her father's hand—the scorpion which had stung that once noble nature to madness.

'O my father, my lost and erring father,' she cried, in an hour when her fear became almost conviction, 'would to God that I could bear the burden of your sin! 'Twas I who tempted you; it was my vile jealousy that urged you to despair and guilt. Let the avenging rod fall heaviest on me. O God, pity and pardon him, Thou who hast promised pardon and pity for the darkest sin!'

That there might be pardon even for this last and most hideous sin of blood-guiltiness, Naomi firmly believed; but could there be forgiveness for a sinner who added the sin of hypocrisy to his darker crime, and held his head high among men when it should have been bowed in the dust under the burden of his shame? Could there be pardon for a sinner who kept the secret of his guilt, and pretended to lead other men along the shining path to heaven? No, assuredly. That smooth-faced hypocrisy—the sin for which man's Teacher and Redeemer reserved

His most scathing denunciations—must treble the infamy of the darker guilt it masked, and render pardon impossible. To the sinner who repenteth pity and peace had been freely offered; but what mercy was ever promised to the Pharisee who, under the semblance of exceptional piety, concealed a deeper infamy than the worst act of the despised publican?

These thoughts were in Naomi's mind as she sat in her narrow deal pew, in the soft June twilight, listening to her father's preaching. The chapel was full to suffocation, for this was one of those meetings which the people of Combhaven particularly affected; a service in which Joshua Haggard was expected to surpass himself, and in which Satan—so often and so directly appealed to as to seem an actual member of the congregation—was to be worsted and driven forth in confusion by the minister's eloquence. Some even went so far as to call these evening services 'devil-hunts.' The part which the congregation took in them was not altogether negative or quiescent. There were times when eager spirits assumed an active share in the proceedings—when from smothered sighs, and head-shakings, and hollow groans, as of inward and bodily disorder, the convulsed auditor was moved to speech, and poured forth his Satanic experiences before a hushed and awe-struck congregation. Joshua did not encourage or favour these lay utterances, and his powerful influence and vigorous eloquence did much to hold his flock in check; but he could not always dam the flood of inspiration.

'You're a powerful praycher, Muster Haggard,' observed a weather-beaten old fisherman, whose rambling discourse Joshua strove to arrest, 'but when a hignorant man feels he's gotten the Holy Sperrit inside un, he ain't goin' to be cut short before he's had his say. Edication goes for nothin' with the Sperrit. He don't mind grammar.'

Upon this particular evening the flock had been content to express its feelings by means of groans and sighs, and brief ejaculations of a self-abasing character. Joshua stood in his square deal pulpit, with an open Bible on the green-baize cushion, and preached of erring humanity and man's darling sins. His sermons were always extempore, and had of late been obviously without plan or method—a change for the worse, which Naomi was conscious of, but which had scarcely been perceived by the flock, that congregation being satisfied with strong language and a flow of rugged eloquence, without looking too nicely for logical precision or directness. Joshua turned the leaves of his Bible, and seemed to draw new ideas from the page he glanced at.

He had been preaching longer than usual, though his sermons were apt to be long, and the twilight deepened as he stood in his pulpit, leaning forward with his elbow on the desk, and the other hand nervously turning the leaves of the Bible, which there was now scarcely light enough for him to see. He looked pale as ashes in that gray light, but his large dark eyes gleamed with a sombre fire as they wandered round the upturned faces of his flock. Sometimes his eyes lingered wistfully on the pew where Naomi sat, and on Cynthia's empty place.

'Yes, my brethren,' he cried; 'yes, fellow-sinners, each has his darling sin. The world sees it not, knows it not. The world honours us—we bask in its smiles and favour. Men point to us as ensamples of godly life. Yet the darling sin is there, in our heart of hearts; we hug it close—we hide it from every human eye. But in the still night-watches it comes forth like a serpent out of his hole, and rears its venomous crest, and stings us with the horror of our guilt. We call ourselves soldiers and servants of God, yet know that our real master and captain is the devil. Yes, my brethren, the great recruiting sergeant has enlisted us. We have taken the devil's shilling; the image and superscription upon the coin is the image and superscription of Satan.

'Alas, my fellow-sinners! know you how swift a thing it is to fall? The fall of Lucifer himself was but the act and passage of a moment. There was no long deliberation—there was no broad gap of time between heaven and hell. In one hour an angel of light standing near the throne—in the next revolted, fallen, banished, the prince and leader of devils. So too with us the fall is swift, the fall is sudden. We are chosen and elected, called to grace—all our old sins forgiven. This regeneration is the work of a moment. We look back and remember the hour in which the light came down upon us, as at Pentecost.

But we may extinguish this light in blackest darkness—we may lose this divine heritage, forfeit our citizenship in the eternal city; and this extinction, this loss, may be the work of a moment.'

Groans both loud and deep, plaintive feminine sighs, disjointed ejaculations of 'Alas!' and 'Too true!' spoke the convictions of the assembled sinners.

'O my brethren, wretched sinners, grovelling in the dust and ashes of this little world, if at this moment the last trump should sound, and the heavens be rent asunder, and the great Judge appear shining in His unspeakable splendour, calling men to judgment, how many among us could answer to that awful summons without fear and trembling, and the knowledge that eternal death was our just doom? How many would He find in this crowded chapel fit to stand before Him? how many of those blessed ones for whom judgment would mean reward everlasting? Would He find twenty, do you think, or ten, or five? Alas, my fellow-sinners, would He find one?'

He lifted his arms aloft at this solemn question, looking up as if he verily saw that appalling day—

the great white throne, the company of angels, the throng of saints and martyrs, the Divine Judge Himself, in their dazzling glory.

'O, come not yet, awful Judge!' he cried; 'we are not ready. Leave us a little more time to wrestle with Satan, to repent our iniquities, to loosen the bondage of this earthly tabernacle, before we stand naked at Thy throne. Who among all these is prepared to meet Thy summons? Who does not tremble as I do at the thought of Thine anger?'

'Ay, tremble, sinner; quail before the God you have blasphemed!' cried a resonant voice at the end of the chapel. 'Tremble, hypocrite; for the sins of those whom you pretend to teach are white as snow beside the blackness of your guilt!'

There was a sudden commotion in the crowded chapel; every one turned towards the door at the end of the building, from which direction the voice came.

Naomi's heart sank with an appalling dread. Too well she knew that voice, though she had never before heard it raised in those tones of withering denunciation.

'A worthy teacher,' cried Arnold Pentreath, facing the excited congregation, who were all standing up in their pews and staring at him, as he stood conspicuous among the crowd at the door; 'a teacher to call sinners to repentance—a fit exponent of gospel truth—a man whose soul is steeped in hypocrisy, whose hands are stained with blood!'

There rose a chorus of exclamations; and then one of the stanchest of Joshua's followers, a brawny farmer, opened the door of his pew and pushed his way out into the narrow aisle.

'Now look 'ee yere, Cap'n Pentreath,' he said; 'I ain't goin' to stand by and yere Muster Haggard abused. You'll just hold your tongue; and if you're gone mazed, you'll take your madness out o' this yere chapel.'

On this there rose a general cry of reprobation at the Captain's unseemly conduct, Joshua Haggard standing up in his pulpit all the while, looking down at his bewildered flock; firm as a rock, but pale to the lips.

'Come out, come out, all of you, and see the witness I bring against him. You think I accuse him without grounds for my accusation. I have my evidence close by—damning evidence. Let him confront it if he can. Do you know that this man—your teacher and guide—is a murderer, a secret assassin?'

'It's a lie!' roared the man who had last spoken; 'it's a lie, and I'd ram your lying words down your throat if I could get at 'ee!'

'It's the truth, and he knows it. Look at him. He doesn't deny it, you see. Look at your teacher —he is dumb. His eloquence fails him for the first time in his life. He does not fear to insult his God by his lying oracles, but he shrinks from the face of the man he has injured. Come out, Joshua Haggard, and meet your accuser. He is at the door. He is waiting—O, so patiently!—till you come and look him in the face.'

Naomi could just distinguish the sailor's white face in the dim light. He stood above the crowd, raised on the step of the door, the entrance of Little Bethel being somewhat higher than the chapel itself.

All was over, then. The worst an avenging God

could bring to pass had come. Her father was known to others as that which she had in so many an hour of agony suspected him to be. He was known as a murderer. By some means or other the secret had been made known. God's ways are wonderful and mysterious. She had always thought that it would be so. Her lost lover's blood cried aloud for vengeance, and the great Avenger had heard the cry.

At last Joshua spoke, and that firm full voice in which he had so often swayed and moved his flock silenced all ejaculations. Every eye was now turned towards the preacher, and all waited his indignant denial of the charge brought against him.

'I am accused of murder,' said Joshua calmly and deliberately, 'and we are told the witness of my crime is at the door. Let us go forth and meet him. Those who know me best here know whether God ever meant me to be the shedder of my brother's blood. He maketh one vessel to honour, and another to dishonour. My position hitherto has been honour, and you who know me can say whether I have been deserving of any other lot.'

'There is not a better man in the country,' cried

the farmer who had first taken upon himself to be Joshua's champion.

'Nor a more pious—nor a more charitable,' clamoured many voices.

'God, who knows all things,' cried Joshua, lifting up his voice with a sudden burst of passion, 'knows that whatever I have taught in this tabernacle of His I have taught from my heart of hearts. I have travailed for this people. I have loved them and striven for them. I have not cheated them with pleasant words, though my heart yearned towards them. Where others have chastised with whips I have chastised with scorpions; but I have preached the Gospel with a single mind. I have had no thought save to teach and to save. O Lord, if I have been the vilest of sinners, at least in this Thy house I have been a true and faithful servant!'

'Ay, and so ye have, Muster Haggard,' chimed in a chorus of women.

'And now let me go forth to meet my accuser,' said Joshua, opening the door of his pulpit and slowly descending the stair.

Naomi had come out into the aisle. She threw

herself in his way as he passed, and linked her arm through his; and thus linked they came along the narrow space together, the congregation falling back a little to let them pass.

Joshua did not repulse his daughter. He suffered her to hold his arm, seeming scarcely conscious of the contact. His dark deep-set eyes looked straight before him under bent brows; his firm lips were closely set. He looked a man who was ready to confront Satan himself in bodily form.

'Come,' cried Arnold, beside himself with suppressed passion, 'your accuser is not loud or clamorous. He will wait quietly till you go to him. It is I that am impatient to set you face to face.'

Joshua and his daughter were at the door by this time. They came close to Arnold. Naomi almost touched him as the crowd swayed against her. She looked at him with an expression which he never forgot.

'O Arnold, what have you done?' she said piteously, in a low voice.

'My duty to my brother.'

They were outside the chapel in the next moment,

in the clear summer evening. The stars were shining in the pale gray; the great green hills stood up against the cool night sky. All wore its accustomed look of rustic peace. And just in front of the chapel-door four men were standing with a litter, on which there lay a quiet figure covered with tarpaulin.

'Come and look at my witness,' said Arnold, seizing Joshua by the arm and dragging him towards the litter, and bending over it to lift the edge of the covering which shrouded that motionless form.

'Stop,' cried Joshua, with a shuddering movement, 'you need not lift it; I can guess. It is death you would have me look on.'

'Yes, death — the body of the man you murdered; my dead brother, whom you slandered in his unhallowed grave, telling me that he had died the death of the suicide. Hark ye, neighbours,' cried Arnold, turning to the awe-stricken crowd; 'it is my brother — Oswald Pentreath — who lies here, shot through the heart by yonder villain nearly a year ago. God only knows if there is evidence enough to bring him to the gallows; but God knows, and I know, that he did the deed. Before you all I accuse him—

your preacher, your pastor, your example of righteousness—he is my brother's murderer. The corpse lies here, silent witness of the crime. He—your preacher yonder—was seen waiting for my brother close to the spot where that corpse was found, shots were heard by the witness who saw him, and my brother was never seen after those shots were fired—never seen; he was lying at the bottom of the old shaft, murdered, and flung there to rot forgotten and unknown. And the murderer looked me in the face, and told me my brother was a coward and had slain himself. If earthly justice cannot touch him, if human ingenuity cannot bring this crime home to his door, may God's justice punish him as never man was punished by mortal avenger! May Heaven make his lot more bitter than the hardest doom man's inhumanity ever devised for his fellow-man's torture!'

'Take your corpse to the dead-house,' cried Joshua, with a contemptuous calmness, as if those passionate threats of Arnold's passed him by like the wind, 'and make your complaint to the coroner. It is his business to find out the cause of your brother's death. All here know that I saved Oswald Pentreath's life at the peril of my own. That is my answer to your charge.'

'Ay, that we do!' cried ever so many voices, and the crowd turned angrily upon Joshua's accuser. 'We all remember how he saved the young Squire that stormy day four year ago—risked his life as if it weren't worth a groat, and brought him in alive off the rock when ne'er another would ha' done it. Doant 'ee be afraid, Muster Haggard. Let un try to lay a finger on 'ee!'

'Come home, father, come home,' whispered Naomi, white as death, and trembling so that she could hardly stand, yet with firmness to make her careful for the father who had always been first in her love and reverence—who was first to-night even, when her lover's corpse lay there before her under its dark pall, awful, unsightly, a thing to be thought of with horror.

She held her father by the arm and led him away from that dreadful spot, scarcely able to walk herself, and yet supporting and sustaining him. The crowd followed, as if to protect their minister—followed and congregated round the garden-rails as Joshua went into his house; and Arnold was left alone with his dead and the little group of farm-labourers who had helped him in his hideous discovery.

CHAPTER XII.

AN OPEN VERDICT.

THE claims of the business had kept Judith Haggard away from the prayer-meeting at Little Bethel. She now came out to the door, surprised and alarmed by the appearance of the eager assembly at her brother's heels—still more alarmed by Naomi's pallid face, as the girl led her father into the dimly-lighted passage.

'Why, what in mercy's name is the matter, girl?' cried Judith; 'has your father had a stroke that you hold him like that, as if he couldn't stand without your help—and what brings all the town after him?'

Joshua's fixed eyes and rigid countenance—awfully calm, with a blankness of expression which was like death itself—might have justified the idea that he had lately been struck down by some mortal illness, and was but just emerged from a state of helpless unconsciousness.

'No, Judith,' he answered, with something of his old firmness; 'the visitation is not such as you think, and yet the hand of God is heavy upon me. A calamity has befallen me which you could never have foreseen, bringing shame upon my name and race, making all the days that I have lived here in honour of no avail. Arnold Pentreath has found his brother's body, and accuses me of being his murderer.'

'You!' shrieked Judith, 'you a murderer!—you murder the young Squire, when you were all but drowned in the work of saving his worthless life! If Arnold Pentreath can bring that charge against you, he is a worse man than I should have thought him, knowing the badness of his blood as I do, and expecting as little as I do from any of his worthless race.'

'He has so accused me.'

'But why? On what grounds? Why suppose that his brother was murdered?'

'His body has been found—in the old shaft.'

'His body has been found—but that doesn't prove that he was murdered. He may have fallen into the shaft.'

'Spare us your arguments to-night,' said Joshua, with a weary air. 'We shall know more to-morrow. I am tired and sick at heart, and want rest. I am in God's hands, and He will deal with me as seemeth best to Him. Yes, in the hands of God—not in the hands of men.'

He left them without another word, and went slowly up-stairs to his own room. The crowd had withdrawn quietly by this time, some hastening back to the spot where they had left Arnold and his ghastly burden — others dropping in at the First and Last to discuss the event that had convulsed their peaceful settlement. All were of one mind about Joshua Haggard, and agreed that the accusation brought against him was as wild and foolish as it was infamous.

'I allus said it 'ud be so,' growled old Jabez Long, the fisherman, from his favourite seat in the chimney-corner, where he hung over the smouldering logs even at midsummer. 'I allus said harm 'ud come of pullin' yon puir chap out o' the say. There's never no good comes o' savin' a drowning man. Chuck un back into the water. That's wisdom—t'other's foolishness. Why, ye see this yere chap can't bide quiet in his grave till he's done Joshua Haggard a hinjury. He rises up agen his deliverer like the onclane sperits that come out o' the tombs.'

There was an inquest held next day in the long low-ceiled justice-room at the First and Last. The body of Oswald Pentreath lay at the Grange, and there awaited the visitation of coroner and jury. It lay in the long white drawing-room—that stately saloon which in its air of disuse and solitude had always something of the look of death. Here to-day lay the master of the house—in the dress he had worn when he left it—a ghastly form, only recognisable by the garments that clothed it, and the colour of the soft golden-brown hair. A pocket-book stuffed with bank-notes and the old Squire's watch and seals had been found upon the body, a proof that the assassin's motive had not been plunder.

Brief was the visitation of the jury to that awful chamber. They had heard the evidence of Arnold Pentreath and the farm-labourers who had assisted in the finding of the body. The search had been long and careful. Guided by the statements of Farmer Westall's cowboy, Arnold had gone straight to the old shaft. He had first searched the ground near the pit, and a few yards from the engine-house, under a furze-bush, he had found one of his brother's pistols discharged. The second pistol had been nowhere forthcoming. Then by means of ropes and ladders, and with due precautions against the effect of noxious gases in the disused mine, Arnold and two of the men had gone down the shaft. Their quest was soon ended. Oswald Pentreath lay at the bottom of the shaft with a bullet through his heart. To bring the body out of the mine was a labour of no small difficulty; but time, the men's sturdy willingness to help, and Arnold's inexhaustible energy, conquered all obstacles, and by the time the earliest star was shining in the calm evening sky, Captain Pentreath was alone in the engine-house, keeping guard over his unburied dead, while the men went to the farmhouse to fetch a litter on which to carry the corpse to the Grange.

That dismal walk through wood and lane had

taken a long time. The church-clock was striking ten as the procession entered the straggling village street. The windows of Little Bethel shone dimly, and Joshua's voice was raised in vehement exhortation.

It was the sound of that voice—the impulse of a moment—which led Arnold to enter the chapel, and denounce the man of whose guilt he had no shadow of doubt.

Old Nicholas, the butler, had been one of the witnesses called to identify the body of his late master. He remembered the clothes Oswald Pentreath wore that last day—and he had helped him to put on that coat—and he could swear to the pistol that had been found under the furze-bush. He insisted upon telling the whole story of his master's departure, and his own fears and wonderment when the trunks were brought back from Exeter. The Combhaven coroner was a patient gentleman, accustomed to a long-tongued race, and listened quietly to the butler's statement. Here was a mystery to be unravelled, and there was no knowing whence the first gleam of light might come.

But when Arnold's evidence took the form of an accusation against Joshua Haggard, the coroner stopped him peremptorily.

'I cannot listen to any such speculations, Mr. Pentreath, to the discredit of a man in Mr. Haggard's position.'

'They are no speculations,' answered Arnold hotly. 'They are convictions. Hear what the next witness has to say, and then you will see what reason I have for accusing Joshua Haggard of my brother's murder—though you can never know all the ground I have for certainty—the looks, the words by which that assassin has betrayed his guilt. Why, I ought to have known it the first time he talked to me of my brother! It was clear enough, if I had had eyes to see, or a mind to understand.'

The coroner protested against the irrelevance of such assertions; and then Timothy the cowboy was called, and told over again the story of that August afternoon on which he had seen Joshua Haggard go up to Matcherly Common.

That picture of the man standing by the door of

the engine-house as if watching for some one impressed and puzzled the jury, but it could not shake them in their conviction that Joshua Haggard was a good man—a man who had taught and reproved them for many years, and who had always dealt honourably with them in temporal matters—a man whose weights were true as the sundial on the church-tower, and whose goods were of the best quality. That such a man could commit a base and cowardly crime savoured of impossibility. Witchcraft alone could account for such a monstrous thing.

'He couldn't ha' done it unless he wur bewitched,' said one of the deliberants when the jury took counsel together.

'Who knows if that young wife of his didn't bewitch him,' argued another. 'There's many 'as marked a change in him from the time she came among us. His thoughts seemed to be roving like, half his time, and he stared at you, skeared like, if you spoke to him sudden, and he got careless about his business. You never found him behind his counter.'

'Joshua Haggard is not the man to hurt a

wurrum,' said a third juryman. 'He used to come and sit beside my puir old missus when she was down with her last illness, and read to her by the hour together, and she looked up to him as if he'd been a saint. I'll agree to no verdick that throws any blame on Muster Haggard.'

'Who wants to bring a verdick agen Muster Haggard? But we mun come to some sort o' verdick, maunt we?'

'Make it accidental death, can't 'ee?'

'But he couldn't a got throwd down the shaft by accident.'

'He might have fell in, mightn't he?'

'Ah, but who was it shot him?'

'He might ha' shot hisself fust, and just had strength enough left to throw hisself down th' old shaft.'

The discussion waxed warm after this, but the jurymen were finally agreed that Oswald Pentreath had been murdered by some person or persons unknown.

Arnold went to the coroner directly the inquest was over, and asked for a warrant to arrest Joshua Haggard.

'My dear sir, it is quite out of the question. There is no evidence upon which I can issue a warrant.'

'Not the fact that the man was seen there, hiding in the engine-house, waiting for my unhappy brother. Is that no evidence?' cried Arnold indignantly.

'There is no evidence that he was hiding—there is no evidence that he was waiting for your brother. The mere fact of his being seen at that place a short time before the firing of the shots amounts to nothing, even if we could be sure those shots the cowboy heard were the shots that killed your poor brother. Joshua Haggard is a mystic, a fanatic, a man who spends half his life wandering in solitary places. I have often met him on the hills and commons. There is nothing strange in the fact of his being seen up yonder that day. Then again, there is an absence of all motive.'

'I beg your pardon,' said Arnold eagerly. 'There was a motive, and a strong one; but there are reasons why I could not speak of this motive just now in open court. It involves error—though not actual guilt—on my brother's part.'

He told the coroner the story of Oswald's attachment to Mrs. Haggard, and the meeting between them that afternoon.

'We have no evidence that Mr. Haggard knew of that meeting,' said Mr. Penruddock, who was much disinclined to make himself odious to all chapel-going people by an unwise arrest of Joshua Haggard.

'We have the evidence of his presence at that spot—at that hour.'

Arnold argued the matter, but in vain, and left Mr. Penruddock, of Wrinkles Close, with the idea that a rustic coroner was the most inept and useless of officials.

Once more Naomi heard the old church-bell tolling dismally in the afternoon sunlight. Again she saw the funeral train wind slowly round the curve of the hill, the same wind-tossed plumes—for even in this June weather the breeze blew fresh from the western sea—the same solemn figures and black horses and poor pomps and vanities of earthly pride; and this time she turned from the shrouded window with the heart-sickness of despair, and cast herself upon the ground, and tried to shut out the light of day, and prayed for death as the one issue and release from her miseries.

They were carrying him to his father's grave—her murdered lover—slain by her father's cruel hand, and slain at her prompting. Had she never put that fatal letter in her father's hand, this thing would never have been. Oswald would have gone his way in peace to a new world and repentance, perchance, and quiet days, and Joshua Haggard would have known nothing of that stolen farewell.

'Half the guilt is mine,' she cried; 'let me bear all the punishment! God be merciful to my misguided father, maddened by jealousy and wounded love! O God, charge not against him his sin that day!'

She had not been alone with her father since that night in the chapel. They had sat at the same board, and she had looked in his face, which told no story of fear or agitation. He had gone about his business with quiet regularity; taught in his school, visited his sick, read and exhorted as of old—yes, even while the inquest was being held at the First and Last, and all his flock were in a state of wildest emotion on their pastor's behalf. There had been a crowd of Joshua's people about the door of the justice-room, a crowd that gave vent to its indignation in a half-smothered way as Arnold Pentreath went in and out of the court. The feeling that their pastor was being persecuted for his faith was strong among them. This accusation of Arnold's was too wild to be believed even by the accuser. It was a lying invention of Satan, designed to put this faithful flock to shame. This feeling pervaded the village, and wherever the minister went he received some new proof of his popularity. Women ran out of their cottage-doors as he passed by, and clasped him by the hand, and offered him their sympathy in this great trial. He shrank somewhat from these demonstrations of feeling. 'Let me bear my own burden,' he said. 'It is not too heavy for me.'

And then when he was alone he clasped his hands in prayer and cried, 'O Lord, reward these people for their affection and their trustfulness, for I can only bring shame upon them. I have built up a temple to Thine honour, and pulled it down, and abased and ruined Thy holy place with mine own hands. I have given Thee half my heart, and sold the other half to the devil. Let these people whom I have loved and taught suffer no loss because of my iniquity. Let their faith endure steadfast to the end, though my life prove a lie.'

Never had there been such a funeral as that of the young Squire of Pentreath Grange. The old churchyard was filled with all the inhabitants of Combhaven, and a crowd of strangers from outlying hamlets among the hills and tiny fishing villages along the rocky coast. This God's acre lay on the side of a hill, and was a place of ups and downs, beautified by many a fuchsia-shaded tomb, and by myrtles that had grown into trees—a sheltered and pleasant spot, hidden from the sight of the sea, but not so remote that the murmur of the waves might not serve as a lullaby for quiet sleepers under the ferny turf.

Arnold Pentreath stood by the open vault, pale and haggard, and with a countenance which grief had made rigid as marble. He was quite alone in his place by the coffin—chief and only mourner.

There was some sympathy felt with him, yet less than would have been given but for that accusation brought against Joshua Haggard. This the Little Bethelites could not pardon. False and monstrous as the charge was, it had inflicted disgrace upon their sect. It was a fact that would be remembered and recorded against them in days to come—a dark tradition to be magnified and distorted by their enemies.

That last ceremonial completed—and O, how brief and hasty a business it seems to the mourner who feels that this is the last!—the coffin placed in its stony niche, for worms to invade and toads to squat upon, and damp and mildew to disfigure—a place of decay and loathsomeness for evermore—Arnold walked slowly away from the churchyard, sick at heart, loathing the faces of his fellow-men. He would not go back to the lych-gate where the coach was waiting for him—would not be shut up again in the Barnstaple undertaker's musty chariot, to hide his grief behind a cambric handkerchief, and so be conveyed slowly along the straggling village street, the principal feature and object of interest for the assembled multitude. He left the churchyard by another gate that led up to the hills—the wild lonely hills, where he could hug his sorrow, and be alone with his baffled vengeance and his passionate grief.

That was the sting—to know his brother's murderer, to have no shadow of doubt as to the assassin, and to be powerless to strike. Conscience had its scorpions, no doubt, and Heaven held in reserve its lash for the hypocrite and murderer; but this was not enough for the brother who had loved his brother. Human nature in its weakness and narrowness of vision yearned for personal vengeance. Arnold wanted to bring this man to the gallows—to be the instrument of his direct and immediate punishment. Nothing less could satisfy his wounded love. His brother's ashes cried to him for vengeance.

One consideration only came between him and this hunger for swift revenge. He remembered that appealing look of Naomi's. His Naomi—his most noble among women—the woman he had hoped to win in days to come—the woman he had pictured in the fair future sitting at his board, ruling his household, making life sweet and honourable for him.

Could he ever hope to win her now? In his own mind he dissociated her altogether from her father's guilt. She was no less pure in his eyes because her father's hands were stained with blood. He was, even in his direst anger, willing to believe that Joshua's crime had been an act of jealous madness, and not the deliberate guilt of a criminal nature.

He could understand now why Naomi had forbidden him to hope, while her looks and tones told him he was dear to her. She had known or suspected her father's guilt. This would account for that deep melancholy which no hopeful utterances of his could dispel.

And if he brought Joshua Haggard to the gallows? What then? Was it not to destroy utterly the woman he so reverenced, the woman he fondly loved? Could Naomi survive so deep a shame, so deadly an agony; or, surviving it, could she have any feeling but hatred for the man who had brought shame and suffering upon her? He remembered that agonised appeal in the chapel,

'Arnold, what are you doing?'

And he had answered her coldly; though that

answer meant the destruction of those new hopes which had been so dear to him. He knew her well enough to be very sure that she would cling to her father till death; stand beside him on the gallows, were it possible, and be true to him after death. To hunt Joshua to his doom as he meant to hunt him must be to lose Naomi for ever.

'Be it so,' he cried. 'What is my happiness, or her peace, that I should put it in the balance with my brother's blood? I have one duty to perform; clear—direct—inexorable. Let me do that, and then go back to the old rough life at sea, and forget that I ever dreamt of being happy on shore.'

CHAPTER XIII.

JOSHUA STOPS HIS WATCH.

LITTLE BETHEL was crammed to suffocation on the Sunday that followed the burial of Oswald Pentreath. Not only had the flock assembled in fullest force to hear their pastor improve the occasion, and enlarge upon the evil that had been wrought against him by the Philistine, but many who were not of Joshua's sect had been drawn to his tabernacle by curiosity. They wanted to see how the man would bear himself under circumstances so trying to manly fortitude.

The flock were not disappointed in the demeanour of their minister. Never had Joshua conducted his simple service with greater dignity. His prayers, those eloquent extemporary supplications modelled upon the theology of William Law, yet, with something of Jeremy Taylor's florid warmth in their colouring, carried his congregation along with him like rushing waters down which a fleet of frail boats are driven tumultuously, knowing not whither they drift. It was by his eloquence in prayer chiefly that Joshua had established his power over his flock. He elevated their souls by his own enthusiasm; they felt themselves raised to a spiritual height which of themselves alone they could never have obtained. They heard their cares and sorrows, their petty doubts and difficulties, their failures and shortcomings and evil acts laid at the foot of the great Throne, with such appeals for pardon and pity as their dull minds could never frame, their uneloquent lips never utter. Joshua took them up in his arms, as it were, and held them at the feet of their Saviour, and called down the eternal mercy for them. He used the Scriptures for their benefit, as a skilful barrister uses precedents for the extrication of his clients. He found bounteous promises that they had never dreamed of in those familiar words of Holy Writ, covenants and pledges of grace and mercy. He held a golden key, with which he opened the treasury of Heaven, and brought forth promises and favours for his people.

To-day his prayers took a tone of deepest self-humiliation. He laid himself prostrate before offended Heaven, and there was none of the exultant pride which the flock expected to discover in his supplications, no thanksgiving for an unsullied conscience and a soul clear of offence, for rectitude which could laugh to scorn the revilings of the evil-minded. It was the publican and not the Pharisee who stood up to pray in that rural temple.

The hymn he chose was of a gloomy cast—but all his ministrations had of late been of a gloomy character. When he went up into the pulpit, and looked round at the upturned faces, and slowly opened his Bible, there was a hush of expectancy. It was thought that his text would have some bearing on the strange event of the past week, and that in his sermon he would take occasion publicly to declare the falsehood and iniquity of the charge that had been brought against him.

But when he had given out the text, with his usual deliberate distinctness, there was a general sense of disappointment—the verses he had chosen seemed to have so little bearing on the subject which filled the public mind.

'In those days they shall say no more, The fathers have eaten a sour grape, and the children's teeth are set on edge. But every one shall die for his own iniquity.' Only Naomi understood the meaning of those words of assurance. For each the burden of his own sin; the assassin's innocent children were to have no portion in the shame and agony of his guilt. Upon this text Joshua Haggard enlarged with more than his accustomed power. Very awful was the picture which he painted of the sinner's earthly doom, the slow agonies of conscience, the shameful shrinking from the face of his fellow-men, the caresses of his children stinging him like the sting of serpents, the reverence and obedience of his household a mockery and a reproach—the light of day intolerable, the sun a burden, the quiet night accursed. And when from this picture of the sinner's suffering on earth he turned to the contemplation of his punishment hereafter, the vision assumed a darker and more terrible aspect. Before the titanic tortures of that land of shadows, earth's puny torments shrunk to the sting of buzzing summer flies as measured against the venom of the cobra or the rattle-snake. Joshua conjured up those visions of horror with a a strange uncanny power, as if the fiend had lifted the corner of hell's curtain, and showed him the fiery gulf behind. He dwelt on these terrors with a gloomy relish, and spoke of hell and doom with a familiar knowledge, as if he had steeped his soul in the fires of Pandemonium.

'But for the sinner's children,' he cried at last, withdrawing his mind, as by an effort, from this contemplation of the nethermost pit, 'they shall go free, Heaven will not lay upon them the burden of a father's sin. He shall perish, he shall go to his doom, but they shall remain scathless. On earth, perchance, their portion may be shame and suffering, for earth's judgments are lying judgments; but God is righteous, and will keep this promise, and will adjust the balance.'

Coming out of chapel, amidst the crowd, Naomi found herself close to a stranger who was talking of her father.

'I can believe anything of this man now I've heard him preach,' he said.

'Why?' inquired his companion.

'Because I am very sure he is a madman.'

'I don't see that,' said the other, startled by the assertion. 'His sermon was violent and gloomy, but sane enough.'

'No sane man ever preached as that man preaches, and you may take my word for it.'

Here the crowd parted Naomi from the speaker, but what she had heard impressed her deeply. It was hardly a new thought which was thus abruptly presented to her. The change in her father had inspired her with fears, to which she had hardly dared to give their actual form. Who was to discriminate between perpetual gloom, moody silence, an unbroken reserve, and the tokens and indications of a mind distraught? That her father's whole character had undergone an alteration since the day of Oswald Pentreath's disappearance, she well knew. Was it not possible that, on that day, the clear light of reason was darkened for ever? From that fatal hour he had broken loose from all old ties—from children and wife, and friends and business—he had been like an owl of the desert, a pelican in the wilderness.

But even with the horror of the thought there came a blessed sense of relief. If reason had left him in the hour of temptation, if the light was quenched before he did that fatal deed, her father was not accountable for his sin. It was not with his whole mind that he had broken the Divine Law. The clouded brain had not taken the measure of the act.

This offered a way out of her deepest sorrow. Dreadful as earthly penalties might be—shameful, intolerable, revolting—it was Heaven's anger she most dreaded for the father she so devotedly loved. Sure of God's pardon and pity for the sinner, she could see him perish on the scaffold with only earthly sorrow, with only sense of earthly suffering and loss; secure of a fair hereafter, a glorious meeting in a land of rest and peacefulness, where the red robes of repentant sinners were to be washed whiter than snow.

Awful, then, as this thought of mental alienation

was, there was comfort in it. She could cling closer to her afflicted father, pitying and pardoning him; full of remorse for her own share in his suffering, ascribing to herself half his guilt.

'If I had but spared him the knowledge of that letter, Heaven might have spared me this anguish,' she thought.

Joshua was absent from the family board at the two-o'clock Sunday dinner, an uninteresting repast of cold provisions, which James Haggard regarded as one of the privations and trials of his career. Other people in Combhaven rioted in hot joints and savoury potatoes, reeking with unctuous grease and gravy, followed by huge fruit pie or pasty, and perchance a bowl of cream.

'I don't call it honouring the Sabbath to sit down to a worse dinner than on a work-a-day,' Jim remarked argumentatively. 'And all that Sally may sit in a corner of our pew and breathe hard all through the sermon.'

'Eat your dinner, and be thankful,' said aunt Judith severely; 'or leave it, and hold your tongue. I wonder you can be so base-minded as to think of your meals at such a time, with such affliction come upon your house as we've had to bear.'

'Do you mean Captain Pentreath bringing that charge against father?' asked Jim contemptuously. 'I'm not such a fool as to fret about that. Any lunatic might accuse us of murder, or arson, or high treason, or gunpowder plot. Poor Pentreath's head's been turned by finding his brother at the bottom of Matcherly mine. I was over at the First and Last when the inquest was going on, and heard everybody saying that it was worse than madness to lay such a crime at father's door. There's not a man in Combhaven would believe a word against father.'

'It would be hard if they would,' retorted Judith, 'after the life your father has lived among 'em all these years, and no one able to bring a reproach against him, unless it was for foolishness in marrying a silly girl for the sake of her pretty face.'

'I never saw any silliness in Cynthia,' said Jim; 'and for my part I wish she was home again. I miss her pretty face, though it was sad enough for the last twelvemonths, goodness knows. I don't think we any of us made her too happy.'

'She's a deal better away,' replied Judith, with a sour look. 'She turned your father's thoughts from his duties, and never brought anything but trouble into this house. Let her stop with friends of her own station, if she has any.'

'Ain't it rather like turning her out of doors to let her stop away so long?' asked Jim.

'I didn't know it was a son's place to find fault with his father's doings,' said Judith. 'Your father's the best judge of his duty to his wife, I should hope. It isn't for us to interfere. He didn't ask our leave when he brought her home, and it's not likely he'd want our leave to send her away.'

'It's a pity things couldn't go smoother, anyhow,' pursued Jim persistently; 'for she's a pretty little thing, and a good little thing, that would never do harm to any one.'

'That's all you know, Mr. Clever. Perhaps you'll be kind enough to keep your opinion till you're asked for it. Why don't you eat your dinner, Naomi?' inquired Miss Haggard sharply. 'It's as good a bit of beef as ever was cooked, and I suppose *you're* not too dainty to eat cold meat on the Sabbath?'

'I'm not hungry, aunt,' said Naomi.

She had been sitting with her plate before her, making no attempt to eat, hearing her aunt and brother talking, but in nowise understanding them. Her thoughts were with her father in his lonely room. He had pleaded a headache, and gone quietly up to his bedchamber when he came in from chapel. How was he bearing his burden? Without consolation, without sympathy. Yes, verily without human sympathy; but for this believer, even in his depth of guilty despair, there still remained a pitying Ear that would listen to his groaning, and take account of his anguish. The Friend of sinners would not be deaf to his cry.

'I think I'll go up-stairs and see how father is, and if he want's anything,' said Naomi, rising from her seat at the table.

'If I was you, I wouldn't go bothering and disturbing him,' said Judith, with her accustomed tartness; 'but of course you can do as you like about it.'

This was an indirect order not to go, but for once in her life Naomi disobeyed, and went straight to Joshua's room.

She knocked, but there was no answer, and she went in quietly, hoping to find her father asleep.

He was sitting in front of the open escritoire, his arms folded, his eyes bent upon the ground. He did not stir, or look up at his daughter's entrance, nor even when she came close to him and laid her hand gently on his shoulder.

She stood for a few moments in silence, waiting for him to take some notice of her; but he sat like a statue, and never lifted his eyes from the ground.

'Dear father,' she began, in a low and tender voice, as she would have spoken to him had he been lying ill, at death's door, 'I was obliged to come to you. I could not bear to think of you alone and unhappy. Dearest, it is a heavy affliction that has fallen upon us, but not heavier than we can bear. Father,' sinking on her knees beside his chair, and putting her arms round him, 'if your guilt is deep, I am guilty too. I sinned grievously when I gave you his letter. I suffered my evil passions to get the better of me. My heart was full of hatred and rancour. Let us repent, and seek for mercy together. We both have sinned.'

'The letter,' muttered Joshua, with a bitter laugh, 'the letter was not so much. I saw him hold her in his arms and kiss her—saw her yield herself up to a love that was stronger than honour or duty, or her love of God—saw her folded to his heart under Heaven's all-seeing eye.'

'It was my fault, father. But for that letter you would never have known of that last meeting. It was but a stolen farewell, and they both meant to do their duty. They were so young, and had erred for want of thought.'

'They were thoughtful enough to plan secret meetings—thoughtful enough to deceive me. And I believed her purest among women—free from all taint of sin. Do not speak of her—or of him. They sinned, and have reaped the fruit of sin. "The wages of sin is death."'

'Father, we have sinned grievously, you and I; and we can have no hope of mercy unless we repent,' said Naomi, horrified at Joshua's hardness of tone, which implied an unconsciousness of the weight and measure of his crime.

'My life has been one long atonement. I

have laboured always in the work of salvation.'

'But by one sinful act all might be undone—in one dark hour the labour of a lifetime might be lost,' urged Naomi.

Her father made no answer.

'Dearest, will you not kneel and pray with me?' she pleaded. 'Will you not help me to lift this burden from my soul? I am weary with the weight of my sin. I loved him, and yet betrayed him to you. O, it was the act of a Judas! *He* must have loved his master. It was jealousy that made him a traitor. Father, if you cannot be sorry for your sin, be sorry for mine.'

In vain; the brooding eyes were never lifted from the ground. Naomi looked up into the rigid face. Yes, there was an expression there as of light quenched, at least a temporary aberration. He was not listening, he was not following her.

He sat for some time thus, Naomi still kneeling by him and watching him, but in silence. Then he stretched out his hand to the open Bible that lay upon his desk, and began to read.

'Leave me, my dear,' he said; 'I am better alone.'

'I would so much rather stay with you, dear father. I will not disturb you.'

'Go, dear; I wish to be alone. I have to command my thoughts. It will be time for chapel presently.'

'I will go then, dear father. But while we are alone, let me say one thing.'

'I am listening.'

She put her arms round his neck, and rested her head on his shoulder.

'You know how I loved Oswald, father, to the last, even after his heart had gone away from me. But I told you then, as I tell you now, you were always first and dearest, always the object of my highest reverence and love. That could never change in me. No act of yours could lessen my love, no affliction Heaven could bring upon you could lower you in my esteem. Remember that always, father. Come what may, I am your loving daughter to the end!'

With this assurance she left him, a little more at peace with herself for having thus spoken.

The afternoon service was gone through very quietly. Joshua had a subdued and weary air, as if worn out by the effort of the morning. The congregation were less alert and exalted in their piety, as was natural in people who had dined heavily, and given way to fleshly snares in the shape of too-substantial pastry. Even the hymns had a slumberous tone, and acted as lullabies upon some elder members of the flock whose feeble knees were an excuse for a sitting posture.

After service, Joshua taught for half an hour in his school, and said a few earnest words to the young men of his adult night-school, a class in which he had taken a special interest. They were very touching words, and well remembered afterwards.

Joshua was absent from the tea-table as he had been from the dinner-table. His headache was worse, he told his sister, and he was going to lie down. Naomi had an evening Scripture class to attend to after tea, a task that would occupy her for about an hour. She went to this duty at half-past six o'clock, while Judith enjoyed the one Sabbath luxury which she permitted herself, a half hour's nap in the chintz-covered armchair by the best parlour window, screened from the gaze of passing pedestrians, going by at the rate of one in ten minutes, by the graceful droop of the well-starched curtain.

Joshua was alone, sitting by the escritoire, as he had sat when Naomi went to him in the afternoon. He had locked the door, determined to be free from all intrusion—free even from his daughter's pitying love. He wanted nothing between him and that awful solitude in which he had lived of late—the isolation which a mind unhinged makes for itself.

He sat thus till the twilight thickened and the pages of his open Bible grew dim. Even in the troubled state of his brain—a trouble which had been growing for months—that book was his rock of defence, his sheet-anchor. He looked into those pages for justification, for assurance of grace and redemption, and he seldom looked in vain. If he had sinned, had not David sinned also, and yet retained his exalted place in the love of God and men? Was he to humble himself more than David humbled himself? Had David ever ceased to be King, and Priest, and teacher, chief and supreme among the people? If *he* had fallen, had not Peter also fallen, and yet received that divine commission which gave him charge of Christ's flock?

'I will preach the Gospel and teach men while I have breath,' protested Joshua, laying his hand upon the sacred book. 'What have the burdens on my conscience to do with my teaching? What does it matter that I know myself a sinner if I can expound the word of God? He has given me a gift, and I will use it—to the uttermost and to the last. If this is to be a hypocrite, my hypocrisy shall go with me to my grave.'

This was the summing-up of his position in one of his calmer moods; but his mind was not always so clear, or his views so fixed and resolute. There were moments to-night, as he sat in the summer dusk while the shadows grew and deepened in the lonely old-fashioned room, grotesque shadows of familiar things which he had known from childhood—there were intervals in which his brain grew clouded, and past and present were alike dim and distorted. His thoughts flashed far and wide like the erratic gleams of a lantern—now alighting upon some picture of the past, now plunging into the dark gulf of the future. He saw himself as he had been at the outset of his laborious career—eager for self-sacrifice, careless of all worldly loss, sustained by an enthusiast's exaggerated hopes, and an enthusiast's indifference to suffering. He had laboured, and had been plenteously rewarded. He had been a wandering light shining in dark places and forgotten corners of the earth, and had brought many lost sheep home to the fold. Then his father had died, and he had been called back to his native place, to find that, after all, he had lost nothing of earthly gain by his constancy, for, despite the old man's threatenings, he had left all to his only son.

This day of inheritance Joshua felt to have been in some measure a time of temptation and falling away. He had turned aside from the desert and desolate places to dwell in a land of fatness. He had been content to serve a few instead of serving many. He had sat down under his vine and fig-tree, and taught one little flock instead of wandering from village to village seeking those whom the Church had forgotten, or cared for with a lukewarm love.

True that he had laboured hard for his flock, walked many miles, stretched his cure of souls to its utmost limits, taught the young, brought the light of education, both spiritual and secular, into many dark places; but he had from this time ceased to be a stranger and a pilgrim upon earth, a disciple who has given up all things for his Master.

Then came his prosperous first marriage, the birth of his children, new ties that bound him to the old home.

How strange and remote those early years seemed as the fitful light of memory shone upon them!

The picture changed. Those peaceful monotonous days were past. He was standing on the Cornish common in the pure sunshine, the great Atlantic glittering in the distance, the sandy knolls and hollows all ablaze with yellow furze, the subtle scent of that golden blossom in the air—standing on the threshold of a new life. Never after that hour was he to be the same man, independent of all human influence. Henceforth he was to be chained to humanity by mankind's most pitiful weakness, an unreasoning love for a weak fellow-creature.

'I verily believe I loved her from that first day,' he thought. 'Her image never left me. She was always before me, sitting in the sunlight, with her drooping hair like pale gold. Can I doubt that Satan set her there for my entanglement and ruin? "His heart shall be heavy for her sake, he shall be so troubled that he shall grow dumb," said the fiend. But I have cheated him of his prey. He has had my heart, and bruised and broken it, but he has not quenched my spirit—he has not silenced me. I have borne my burden and continued to teach and exhort, and will so continue to the end. No snare of the Arch-tempter hiding behind a fair face shall destroy me.'

Then followed a moment of relenting.

'She seemed so innocent, so pure. She was so gentle and obedient, and owned so meekly that she had been tempted, and had sinned in hearkening for a little while to the tempter. O God, there could be no vileness in the soul that looked up at me from those gentle eyes. And I thrust her from me with violence and contumely, and sent her back to servitude and dependence. My wedded wife, the one creature I have loved most on earth!' He clasped his hands, and looked upward in exaltation of mind.

'Surely that was an atonement for my weakness. Surely that was a sacrifice which Heaven must approve. And yet I have known no peace of mind since that day. Heaven has given me no token of approval or forgiveness.'

That intense egotism which is one of the characteristics of a mind off its balance had taken possession of him. He felt himself the centre of the universe. The Bible had been written for him. He stood face to face with his Creator, and felt himself worthy to be saved.

His daughter knocked at the door presently, and asked him if he would not have a light.

'No,' he answered; 'my soul can hold communion with God in the darkness. I am alone, as Elijah was upon the mountain, waiting for the voice of the Lord.'

It was after midnight when he laid himself upon his bed, wearied with meditations in which his brain had been hyper-active. Tired as he was with the long day and its double service, the long evening and its protrated thoughtlessness, he could not easily sleep; and when at last his weary eyelids closed, his slumber was more like a trance than a sleep.

He saw his wife's face looking up at him as she had looked that last day in the lane, pleadingly, piteously, full of grief and love. He saw it more vividly than faces are seen in dreams—saw it close to him as he lay upon his pillow, and was dimly conscious of lying there, and the hour of the night, and that this face was looking at him from afar off, though it seemed so near that he could have stretched out his hand and touched it.

Then came a voice that thrilled him:

'Joshua, Joshua, come to me!'

He was awake and on his feet in an instant. It seemed to him that his waking ears had heard that voice—that it was something more than a part of his dream. He stood listening for some moments, half expecting to hear the cry repeated, and his wife's hand upon his door.

He went to the door, and opened it, and

looked out upon the landing faintly lighted by the stars.

No, the place was empty, the lower part of the house was dark and silent. Nothing had happened. It was only a dream.

'But it is a dream sent by Heaven,' he said. 'I will hearken to it, and go. Yes, my love, I forgive you; I am coming to you. I bring you pardon and love.'

He struck a light from the old tinder-box, lighted his candle, and began to dress himself hurriedly. He had looked at his watch on first rising, wondering to find so little of the night was gone. It was twenty minutes past one o'clock.

Joshua took his watch from under his pillow, lifted the glass, and laid his finger on the hands and stopped them. Only once before in his life had he ever done this thing, and that occasion was the moment of his conversion, the instant in which the divine assurance of his election and calling had been breathed into his soul. At that blessed moment he had stopped his watch that it might for ever record that one hallowed hour. It was the watch he had used as a young man, and was still in his desk: he had never carried it afterwards, and had endured no small inconvenience for the want of it till his father's fine old timekeeper had descended to him as a part of his inheritance.

It was a curious fancy which moved him to do the same thing to-night. He could have given no reason for the impulse, but he obeyed it blindly, and the loud ticking of the watch grew still at twenty minutes past one.

CHAPTER XIV.

JOSHUA'S CONFESSION.

ANOTHER bright June morning; newly-blown roses looking in at the open windows, born, like the butterflies, for a day. Naomi was astir earlier than usual after a sleepless night, full of care for her father. O, if that sweet air of heaven, which is a joy in itself for the happy, could but blow away one's sense of abiding trouble, could but bring the promise of relief! This was what Naomi thought, as she stood at her open window, looking out at the calm hill-tops, from which the summer mists were rising, like a veil slowly unfolded by invisible hands.

She was at her father's door before six o'clock, knocking and waiting his reply with fast-throbbing heart, fearing she knew not what. There was no answer. She felt the floor reeling under her feet. Awful fears seized upon her. She knocked loudly, violently almost, and still no answer. She tried the door with shaking hands, expecting to find it locked, as it had been yesterday evening when she came to inquire about the light; but it yielded under her hand, and she went into her father's room.

It was empty. She looked round with wild eager eyes, almost beside herself in the agony of that great dread. The room was quite empty. The bed had been lain upon; the candle had been left burning, and had burned down to the brazen socket. There was a letter lying on the escritoire, which Naomi seized upon eagerly. It was addressed to herself.

She tore it open, still full of fear; for the letter might reveal some terrible determination. There was another letter inside, sealed, and addressed to Captain Pentreath.

'My beloved Daughter,—I am going to Penmoyle to seek my wife, and shall return to Combhaven no more. My duty there is done. I have taught my people to know the right path. I can give them up into the hands of a new minister. I am going where the darkness has never been dispelled by Gospel light: I am going to find new duties in desolate places. But first I must see my wife. I would pardon and bless her before I go. Do not follow me. My lot is fixed.

'Do not fail to give the enclosed letter, with the seal unbroken, into Captain Pentreath's hands. —Your affectionate father,   JOSHUA HAGGARD.'

Naomi lifted up her heart in thankfulness. He had gone to do no wicked and desperate act. He had gone to seek his wife, carrying with him pardon and love. The ice had melted. Who could tell what healing for mind and soul there might be in the change?

But this letter to be delivered to Arnold Pentreath? Here was a fearful thought. What if it were a confession of her father's guilt—a confession which would put his life in Arnold's power? And Arnold had already shown himself merciless. To withhold the letter would be to disobey her father's express command. To deliver it might be to endanger his life. What was she to do?

She sat by the escritoire with the letter in her

hand, perplexed in the extreme. Then, finding thought useless to show her the way, she fell upon her knees and prayed for guidance, prayed long and earnestly.

She rose from this prayer resolved, whether for good or ill, she would obey her father's behest, and deliver the letter, trusting to God's mercy and her own influence with Arnold for the issue. He had pretended to love her—nay, had loved her—before this fearful discovery of his brother's fate. She must have some power over him still; her pleading must be of some avail. Yes, she would obey her father, and in so doing proclaim her trust in Providence.

'" Let me fall now into the hand of the Lord; for very great are His mercies," ' said Naomi. ' Can I doubt that my father is in God's hands to-day, though men may seem to have the ordering of his fate?'

She lost no time in carrying out her determination, but went back to her room and put on her bonnet, and then ran down-stairs.

She was going out at the street-door when it suddenly occurred to her that her father's absence must speedily be discovered, and would make a commotion in the house if it were in no manner accounted for. So she went to the kitchen, where her aunt was employed in her usual morning duty of giving out provisions for the day's consumption from a rigorously locked store-room.

To her Naomi quietly announced that her father had started early that morning on his way to Penmoyle to see his wife.

'Started early!' cried Judith incredulously. 'Why, the Truro coach doesn't go before half-past seven, and it's not a quarter-past yet. What do you mean by started early?'

'He may have set out to walk part of the journey, perhaps, aunt,' answered Naomi. 'You know how fond he is of walking. He was gone at six o'clock when I went to his room, and had left me a letter to say he was going to Penmoyle.'

'I think he might have written to me,' said Judith, with her offended air. 'If he must needs go off at a moment's notice, throwing all the housekeeping into a muddle — you needn't roast the mutton to-day, Sally; the cold beef will be good enough for us—he might at least have had the civility to address his explanation to me. After keeping his house nearly thirty years it's hard to have such a slight put on me.'

'The beef, mum!' remonstrated Sally; 'there's hardly anything but bones.'

'Nonsense, girl; there's plenty of picking between the bones. And if I've time I'll make a treacle pudding.'

Naomi vanished while the dinner was under discussion. Her heart was very heavy as she went to the Grange. She had not entered the house since the days when she had been Oswald's plighted wife, and the future lay fair before her, full of the promise of happiness. And now there was a thought of horror in the very road by which she went. Twice had her murdered lover been carried along that road; and now he was lying quietly in his grave, and all earthly hopes lay buried with him.

The old house looked peaceful enough in the cheerful morning light. Gardens and shrubberies had been better kept since Arnold's return. The beds and borders were full of sweet-smelling flowers.

The windows were all open, and a handsome red setter—a favourite of Arnold's—was lying in the porch.

Naomi rang the noisy old bell, which was answered after a longish pause by Nicholas the butler, who came across the hall, carrying his master's breakfast on one of those old silver trays which had been kept under lock and key during the Squire's lifetime, but which the less careful sailor had given out for daily use.

At sight of Naomi the old man stopped short, with a startled look.

'Lord, miss, how you skeared me!' he exclaimed.

'Can I see your master, Nicholas?'

'To be sure 'ee can, miss. He's to his break'ust in the blue parlour—the room that was Squire's study, you know; but the harkiteck had it all routed out and painted.'

The butler opened the door of that small room on the left hand of the porch, and ushered Naomi into the presence of Captain Pentreath.

He started up with a cry, half surprise, half welcome, as if to see her only were in itself so glad a thing, that he forgot all the painful circumstances of their meeting. This oblivion lasted but for a moment. His face clouded, and he looked at her deprecatingly.

'Naomi, I have been longing for such a meeting as this. I want to tell you—to make you understand, if I can—that in what I have done I have been constrained by my duty to the dead. Had your father wronged me—that wrong the deepest one man could do another—I would have endured all for your sake; but my duty to the dead is sacred. At the hazard of breaking your heart, with the certainty of losing your regard, I was forced to do what I did.'

'Hush!' she said; 'do not speak of me or my feelings. You have brought great misery upon us— an irreparable shame. It may be in your power to work still greater misery for us. I can but do *my* duty to God and my father. My first duty to both is obedience. I have brought you a letter.'

'A letter?'

'From my father. But before I give it you, promise that you will make no evil use of it, that you will not make his own words the means of destroying him. I cannot tell what he has written. I know that all yesterday his mind was sorely disturbed—that he has been oppressed and troubled in mind for a long time. How can I tell what he has written? Promise me that you will not use this letter against him.'

'I promise,' answered Arnold, with a touch of scorn. 'It is not likely that a letter which your father writes to me of his own free will can prove a weapon with which to strike him.'

He opened the letter, prepared to find an artful and studied composition setting forth the minister's innocence of the crime charged against him, a plausible and subtle defence, such as the ingenuity of a clever and thoughtful man might elaborate at his leisure. The paper almost dropped from his hand as he read the first line.

'Arnold Pentreath, you accused me rightly. It was this hand slew your brother. But the deed was not so basely done as you think. We stood face to face, each with his weapon in his hand. It was what the sons of Belial call an honourable meeting, though my conscience tells me it was murder. He stole my young wife's heart—came between me and the most perfect happiness that Heaven ever vouchsafed to man. I met him with my wife's kiss still warm upon his lip. I had seen them part, mind you, as lovers whose hearts are cloven asunder in parting. I told him that he owed me his life, and he was willing to admit the debt. "My life is of so little value that you are heartily welcome to it," he said; "I have often thought of taking it myself." He had a pair of pistols about him, and proposed that we should fight on the spot; but withdrew his proposal the next moment, remembering that I had no practice in the use of firearms.

'I told him I was willing to set my want of skill against his bad cause. "It is you that are the wrongdoer," I cried; "Heaven will be on my side."

'We fought, and he fell. I was alone with his dead body, and all the horror of my position was suddenly revealed to me. According to my own creed I was a murderer; and in the sight of the world I should stand revealed as a murderer if I were found with this dead man by my side.

'Satan, who had made me blind to the guilt of my act till it was accomplished, now tempted me to the baseness of concealment. I dragged the body to the edge of the shaft and threw it down, and went quickly home, and kept silence about your brother's fate till the day I spoke of him with you.

'I told you that in my opinion your brother had committed suicide. I say still that he flung his life recklessly away. Had he pleaded or argued with me my blind passion might have been subjugated. He put the weapon which killed him into my hand.

'God rest his soul, and pardon my sin!

'I am going forth to a life as desolate as that of St. John in the desert. May God so appoint my punishment here that I may not lose my portion in glory hereafter!   JOSHUA HAGGARD.'

Naomi stood before Captain Pentreath with ashen lips, watching him as he read the letter, praying dumbly all the while, and with that sense of efficacy in her prayers, even in this moment of suspense, as only an implicit faith can experience.

'Thank God!' exclaimed Arnold, giving her the

letter; 'thank God it is not so bad as I believed! This confession has the stamp of truth; and—he is your father!'

No words can tell the depth of tenderness in that little speech and the look that went with it.

Both look and tone were lost on Naomi. Her eyes were rooted to the letter; triumph, gratitude, joy, illumined her face.

'It was not murder,' she cried; 'there was no treachery, no secrecy; they stood face to face—sinners both—blinded, maddened by passion. It was no murder. Father, how could I have wronged you by such base thoughts—I, who have known and loved you all these years? Guilty! yes, I will acknowledge your guilt; but not a treacherous assassin. My God, I thank Thee!'

In days when the first gentlemen of the land asserted their sense of honour and superiority to the common herd by slaying one another in a formal manner the idea of a duel was not so revolting as it is now. Even to Naomi, educated as she had been in a far different creed from the code of honour, the knowledge that her father had stood face to face with his foe, risking his own life against the life he took, was an infinite relief. In horrible nightmare dreams she had seen him, with the assassin's face, creeping stealthily towards his victim. The horrid image had haunted her sleeping and waking; and now that horror was laid at rest for ever. Her belief in this confession of her father's was as implicit as her faith in God.

'Arnold,' she pleaded, with deep humility, as one who asks an almost impossible boon, 'can you ever bring yourself to forgive my erring father?'

'No!' he answered stoutly; 'but I no longer look upon him with loathing. There is one atonement left to him—he can stand face to face with me, as he stood with my brother, and let God judge between us.'

Naomi flung herself at his feet, clasping his hands, as if he held the keys of life and death.

'No, no, no!' she cried; 'you would not be so cruel, so wicked—you, who condemn the shedder of blood!'

'I want the life of the man who slew my brother. So much the better if I can have it in an honourable manner. Yes, Naomi, we will meet as men of honour should, and let the righteous cause win.'

'Arnold,' she cried, 'I thought you loved me.'

The pathos of that cry moved him. He bent over her as she knelt at his feet, resisting his effort to raise her, clinging to his knees in her agony, pleading as only women can plead for the love of their dearest.

'If I thought you loved me, and would give me love for love,' he said, with a sudden change to passionate tenderness, 'I would spare his life; yes, let him go unpunished to the grave; yes, forget that I ever had an only and beloved brother. It is a mean offer, a miserable bargain, proving me selfish, dastardly; but I am human, and I love you. My love, my only love, answer me.'

'Can you forgive me for being my father's daughter?'

'When I believed the worst of him I loved you, and held you unsullied by his guilt.'

'You must forgive him, Arnold. You would forgive him if you knew as much as I do. He was not in his right senses that awful day. I saw him go through the wood. Yes, I was there watching for him, fearing evil. His face has haunted me ever since. It was the face of a madman. It was my sin that caused all. Yes, Arnold, mine. You do not know how vile I am. I gave my father the letter your brother wrote to my stepmother! A lover's letter, full of despairing love. *That* maddened him, as it had maddened me. He was not in his right mind that day. He has never been the same man since—gloomy, austere, set against those he had loved before. You cannot conceive how great a change there has been in him. We who have lived with him know and feel it. On my knees here, before God, I do not believe that my father was responsible for his acts that day.'

Arnold raised her from her knees, and put her in the armchair by the open window. She was almost fainting, but the brave spirit struggled with bodily weakness.

Arnold paced the room for a little while deep in thought.

'What am I to do, Naomi?' he asked at last. 'I love you—would lay down my life for you; but

I owe a duty to my brother. That is a solemn charge. He loved me—was so good to me. I have his letter summoning me home, full of affection, overflowing with generosity. What am I to do, Naomi? Counsel me, if you can. You loved him?'

'Loved him? Yes; it was my love that made me mad with jealousy; it was my love that rose up against him and destroyed him. If you must have a life for his life, take mine. Yes, Arnold, take mine. I am most guilty. It was my jealousy that killed him.'

'Naomi, we are all most miserable. I can do nothing; I feel myself tied and bound. Either way there is wrong and misery. I love you, and am miserable in loving you. I have my brother's death to avenge, yet cannot bring myself to injure your father. O my love, my love! your sad accusing face has haunted me ever since that night when you turned and looked at me at the chapel-door. What can I do?'

'Forgive,' said Naomi solemnly; 'that is what the Gospel teaches us—to forgive our enemies, even the enemies who have injured those we love. We can never err in being merciful. "How often shall my brother sin against me, and I forgive him? Till seventy times seven." That must mean pardon for wrongs man thinks unpardonable.'

'You can teach me to believe anything, Naomi. I am like a child in your hands.'

'May God teach you to judge and act wisely! He will not inspire you with thoughts of vengeance. He has said, "Vengeance is mine, I will repay." My unhappy father has suffered for his sin, and will continue to suffer till death brings him peace; but I know in my heart that God will forgive him.'

'And if God can forgive, erring man should not be obstinately unforgiving. That is what you would say, Naomi. We have an illimitable faith in God's capacity to pardon, yet find it so hard, sinners as we are, to forgive a fellow-sinner. It is a dark problem.'

'Pray that you may understand God's will, Arnold. He will lead and uphold you.'

'No; earthly passion will sway me. It is my love for you urges me to forgive your father.'

'I would have you act from a higher light. I

will leave you to seek a better guidance,' Naomi answered, with gentle reproachfulness.

She felt that her father was secure from any violence of Arnold's after this interview. She left him full of faith that the right guidance would come, that the vengeful spirit which had threatened Joshua with ruin and death would be calmed and appeased. She knew that Arnold loved her; and though all thoughts of herself were vague and secondary at such a crisis of her father's fate, she was glad of Arnold's love, for her father's sake.

CHAPTER XV.

CARRYING PEACE AND PARDON.

Joshua was far upon his road before Naomi had left the Grange. He had walked many miles in the dull gray of early morning, before the shadowy clouds had parted or the stars begun to pale in the saffron lights of sunrise. The energy that sustained him, the eager purpose that bore him on in that beginning of his journey, made him unconscious of time or distance. He had heard Cynthia calling; yes, his wife's cry, piteous and weak, as of one in distress, was still sounding in his ear as he hurried along the well-known road, which seemed just a little strange and dreamlike in the dim gray dawn. He had heard her calling him, and he was going to answer her cry.

'Dearest, I am coming to you,' he repeated inwardly. 'I, who drove you away with undeserved reproaches, am coming to pray for pardon; I, who was cruel, unjust, savage, and inhuman, only because I loved too blindly,—I am coming to ask for pity from the tender heart I wounded. Love, I was mad, and I have suffered for my madness—a long night of suffering. The morning has come, and peace and pardon. My eyes are opened; I see and understand.'

It was only when a sudden faintness made him stagger dizzily, and stretch out his hands to save himself from falling, that he became aware of the hot sun beating down upon his head, and the fact that he had walked many miles.

He was nearly twenty miles from Combhaven. He had crossed the wild craggy hills, and come back mechanically to the coach-road. He was at the top of a long hill, and saw the coach toiling slowly up the white dusty road. He felt all at once that his strength was gone—gone utterly, as if it had left him for ever—and thanked God for the coming of the coach. It seemed by a special providence that he had been brought across those wild hills back to the turnpike-road in time for the passing of the coach.

'If I had missed it I should not have got to

Penmoyle to-night; and my darling is waiting for me,' he said to himself.

There was a vacant place on the seat behind the driver. Joshua hailed the coach, and scrambled into this place before the coachman had time to pull up his horses.

'You shouldn't ha' done that, Mr. Haggard,' remonstrated the man; ' it's dangerous.'

Joshua took no notice. The man's voice sounded far off, as in a dream. The horses went downhill and uphill over the wild yet fertile country, by hills and woods that Joshua knew as well as he knew his Bible. They stopped to change horses in straggling little villages, where he had preached in his young days; and people who remembered those days came out of their houses, and stood looking up at the coach and talked to him. He answered their inquiries and acknowledged their civil speeches mechanically, dimly conscious of their identity. He had a curious feeling of superiority to all these people, as if the universe had been planned for him, and they were only accidents in it, like the great black flies buzzing round the heads of the patient blinkered coach-horses, to whom Providence had given no special mercy except mane and tail.

The time had been—and but a year or so ago—when he would have got down from the coach and peeped into those whitewashed cottages, and had his well-chosen word of greeting or counsel for each old acquaintance. To-day their faces looking up at him were blank and meaningless. The faces of the rabble round Stephen may have looked so to the saint and martyr in his death agony.

Joshua's mind was going on before him. He fancied himself arriving at Penmoyle in the sunset. She would be standing at the gate perhaps, watching for him, as he had found her on that unforgotten afternoon two years ago. He would see the sweet face with the western light shining on it, the soft eyes kindling with love and happiness at sight of him. He had almost forgotten that bitter day of parting, the day when he had driven her into banishment, with more cruelty than Abraham had shown to ill-used Hagar; and it can hardly be said that the patriarch was a pattern to all future husbands in that transaction.

O, how sweet it was to dwell upon that picture of meeting and reconciliation! The burden on his conscience had been cast off since the agony of yesterday. It was verily as if he had laid down his load on the sinners' altar. He forgot all the silent pangs and tortures of the last year, and felt as if a new life of happiness was opening before him. He would carry the lamp of the Gospel into dark places, he would preach by the wayside, as in his youth; he would carry neither purse nor scrip, but wander from village to village and from town to town, in that benighted north country he had read about in the lives of Wesley and Whitfield; or, if it were possible, still farther away, among the absolute heathen of the South Seas.

This was his vision of a glorious future. And she would be with him—his companion, helpmeet, and comforter. It was such a career as this to which she had aspired. Her spiritual nature had been revolted by the trader's petty life—she had sighed to see her husband doing the work of an apostle.

Such thoughts as these were in his mind all through the day. They rose and fell in his brain, wave upon wave, as regularly as the waves of the Atlantic were rising and falling upon the long sandy shore beyond those brown Cornish hills. The day seemed very long to him, for his exaggerated activity of brain made minutes like unto hours. And yet he was ineffably happy. No fear of disappointment at the end of his journey clouded the radiance of his visions. He apprehended no further stroke from an angry fate. God had punished him with the undying worm called conscience, and had heard his prayers and forgiven him. He feared nothing.

It was afternoon when the coach rumbled into the stony street of Truro. Joshua had to be reminded of his fare respectfully by the coachman. He was on the point of hurrying off without paying it.

'Your mind's full of better things, I know, Mr. Haggard,' said the man; 'but I thought you'd like me to remind you.'

'Thank you, Norman,' said Joshua dreamily. 'Yes, my mind was much occupied; pleasantly, though, pleasantly, as one sure of God's bounteous mercy.'

He gave the man a crown for himself. It was half as much as the fare—an astounding donation.

'You may not be driving me again for some time to come,' said the minister kindly.

'Thank'ee, sir. It isn't many behaves as handsomely, and it's always a pride to drive such as you. But don't take it as a liberty if I give'ee one bit of advice. Don't try to get up to the outside of a coach before the horses 'ave stopped. You're in the prime of life, sir, maybe; but you're a good many years too old to do that with safety.'

'Yes, yes, Norman; I shall bear it in mind,' said Joshua, walking away, without stopping at the comfortable inn for 'bite or sup,' as Norman remarked afterwards.

'The fact is the minister is wearing of hisself out,' the coachman remarked to his cronies that night. 'He's got oddish ways with him, and a look as if he didn't half know what's going on round about him.'

CHAPTER XVI.

THE ODOUR OF ROSEMARY.

It happened as Joshua had calculated. The sun was setting as he entered quiet Penmoyle. The walk from Truro had tired him more than he had supposed possible. He could hardly drag himself along the last mile or so of the dusty road, between hedges where the dog-roses and honeysuckle climbed high above his head, and where the foxgloves were opening their purple bells. The salt sea-wind, sweeping over yonder swelling hills, seemed to have lost its refreshing power. He turned his eyes wearily towards the western point—the wild Land's End, with its rocks of many-hued granite, on which the sea-gulls and cormorants were perching in the rosy evening light. The scene was so familiar to him that he could see it all, in that clear vision of the mind, as he turned his gaze westward. Was there anything on this vast earth more beautiful, he wondered, than that wild point of English soil, with the great Atlantic waves for ever beating up against it—an impregnable natural fortress, the rocky seat of dead and gone giants, for ever defying the assaults of ocean?

His thoughts wandered a good deal during these last miles, when his body was racked with the pains of exceeding fatigue. He thought of Nicholas Wild, his old pupil, and the little chapel among yonder hills. The young man had written him long letters, telling him of the rich reward that had crowned his labours, and how he had built a school for the children of his flock. Joshua had been too preoccupied to take any notice of the letters, and the memory of that neglect smote him now as he came nearer his pupil's home.

'Poor Nicholas! he was always faithful and affectionate. We will go and see him, my wife and I,' Joshua said to himself.

At last the old square tower of Penmoyle church rose in its gray severity above the avenue of limes that led to it. Then came the well-known street; the chestnut-grove where the children played at eventide; the inn; the village pump; the cocks and hens, and a vagabond pig picking up unconsidered trifles in the middle of the road; the old yellow wagon turned up on end after a day's usefulness. The sun was still visible—a shining crimson disk on the edge of the western hill.

It was a mere foolishness, no doubt, and Joshua chid himself for so weak a regret, but he felt strangely disappointed when he came in sight of the little green gate before Miss Webling's cottage, and did not see the graceful figure of his wife standing there, just as he had seen her that happy afternoon two years ago, when he had come full of benevolent intentions, and ignorant of his heart's mystery. He had counted on seeing her there. It would have been the natural fulfilment of his dream, it seemed to him, that she should be on the watch for his coming. She had called him, and, by some mystic power beyond the limits of flesh and blood, he had heard her summons. Why was she not watching for him, full of faith in his obedience? Was his sympathy with her stronger than hers with him?

He passed the chestnut-grove. It seemed to him

that the children were less noisy than of old. They were there under the spreading branches, the same boys and girls—the fustian jackets and lavender pinafores, the petticoated little ones, with chubby cheeks and great staring brown eyes. But there was a hush upon the scene. The elder children were congregated in little knots talking. Some of them suddenly perceived him, and there was a curious excitement among them immediately, and much whispering, and some pointing at him with eager fingers; and he could see that they all stopped their talk or games to watch him.

Joshua walked slowly towards the green gate, strangely disappointed and depressed. The windows of the Webling cottage faced south-west, and it was only natural that the spotless blinds should be drawn to exclude such a blaze of sunset; but it gave the house a blank look not the less. The casements offered him no smile of welcome.

Here was a friendly welcome, however, from an unexpected direction. Before Joshua had opened the gate, Mr. Martin, the kind old minister, came hurrying across from his dwelling on the other side of the road, and clasped him by both hands, and looked at him with eyes brimming over with tears.

'God bless you! God sustain and comfort you, my beloved friend!' he cried. 'I was watching for you. O, be composed, my friend, be composed! Such a blessed euthanasia! The precious soul of my Elizabeth was not more spotless or fitter for heaven. Dear friend, let us go in together.'

Joshua turned and looked at him with wild wondering eyes; then wrenched himself suddenly from the old man's friendly grasp, and moved towards the door.

'No, no,' he muttered; 'I don't want you. I am going alone—to see my wife. Cynthia!' he called, as he opened the door. 'Cynthia!' in a louder and more urgent tone—'Cynthia, where are you?'

A fiery impatience had taken hold of him. He could not wait for formalities of any kind. The Miss Weblings would come, and there would be stately greetings, and cake and wine brought out of the wainscot cupboard, and all manner of ceremonies before he could open his arms and clasp his ill-used wife to his heart, and weep over her and be forgiven.

Deborah came out of the kitchen, and took his hands, just as old Mr. Martin had done, and looked at him in the same tearful way.

Were the people all mad here, or was he? Even the children had seemed to look at him strangely.

'Dearest friend,' said Deborah, 'this is a sore trial for all of us. Priscilla has been in hysterics all day; out of one fit into another. Quite dreadful! The feathers we've burnt, and the vinegar, and all to no purpose. She has such a feeling heart.'

It was Priscilla who was ill, then. That's what all this fuss meant.

'I want to see my wife,' Joshua said shortly.

'At once?' faltered Deborah, looking at him timorously.

'Yes, at once; this instant. Have I not come all these weary miles to see her? This instant.'

'O dear sir, what need of impatience? Be calm, I beg you.'

The doors of both parlours were open. Joshua had glanced in and seen that both rooms were empty.

'Where is she?' he asked. 'Up-stairs?'

'Yes, in our spare room,' Deborah answered huskily. 'Let me show you the way.'

'I know it,' he said; and went up-stairs before her.

The narrow corkscrew staircase was close and dark, like the winding stair in a church-tower. Midway Joshua started as if he had been shot, and came to a standstill.

There was a pungent odour of freshly-gathered herbs, a perfume he had not smelt thus, on the threshold of a bed-chamber, since his mother's death.

'My God!' he cried. 'Is it rosemary?'

'Yes,' sobbed Deborah, 'we always use it here. We've a bush in the garden on purpose. The neighbours come and beg a bunch of it when they've a death in the house.'

Joshua staggered up the few steep stairs, lifted the jingling latch of the low wainscot door, and went into the room in which he had slept two years ago, when the new joys and pains of love began to grow in his heart.

That odour of rosemary had forewarned him what he was to see. No living wife, standing on the threshold to greet him, with warm arms ready to be wound about his neck—no sweet eyes lifted shyly to meet his own—no faltering words, or half-broken sobs: only a fair marble statue lying on a white flower-strewn bed, hands meekly folded, violet-veined eyelids closed over wearied eyes—a broken heart for ever at rest.

He stood looking at her for a long time, as it seemed to the heart-stricken Deborah—looking at her with eyes that hung upon that silent beauty in a rapture of despair; then flung up his arms with a sudden gurgling cry, and fell upon the floor beside her bed like a stone.

He remained unconscious for many hours, breathing stertorously, and lying like a log upon the bed where his faithful attendants had laid him. The village doctor had bled him, and administered various orthodox remedies of a severe character, with but little result. Mr. Martin, the good old dissenting minister, stayed with him all through the weary night, which might know no dawn in this world. The spinster sisters were indefatigable, Priscilla waiving her peculiar prerogative of hysterics in her desire to be useful.

The sun had risen, and the birds were singing outside the open casements, when Joshua slowly lifted his heavy lids and looked about him with dim bloodshot eyes.

For some minutes after he had struggled back to consciousness there was a dimness in his brain as well as in his eyes, and he looked at the anxious watchful faces vaguely. Then memory came back with cruel distinctness.

'Tell me—everything,' he said.

'Dear friend,' pleaded Mr. Martin, 'let your mind be at rest for a little while. Repose, dear sir; you have been heavily afflicted, and you have had a stroke of illness which might have been fatal, had God refused to hear our earnest prayers.'

'Tell me about my wife,' urged Joshua vehemently.

'She is at rest. She has gone to her heavenly home. I, who was with her at the last, have no doubt of her calling and election. She was one of God's chosen vessels, with a mind naturally attuned to heavenly things, like that pure spirit, my heavenly-minded Elizabeth, whose deathbed conversations it was my precious privilege to preserve for the edification of many. Yes, she came very near that sainted young woman in the holy simplicity of her nature.'

'What was it that killed her?' asked Joshua, putting aside all these words with a motion of his strong hand. 'Did she die of a broken heart? Was it my ill-usage that caused her death?'

'Your ill-usage, dear friend! Your senses must be wandering. She always talked of you as the best and most honoured of husbands. Ill-usage, and from you! She loved you above all earthly things. Your name was on her lips with her last breath.'

'Yes,' cried Joshua, 'she called me, and I heard her. Give me my watch,' pointing to the chest of drawers where it lay; 'see, I stopped the hands at the moment in which I heard her voice calling to me in a kind of dream—not a common dream, mark you—twice as vivid and lifelike. It was after midnight on Sunday; see, twenty minutes past one.'

'"This is the Lord's doing; it is marvellous in our eyes!"' exclaimed Mr. Martin piously. 'It was at that very hour her spirit took flight.'

'Why was I not told that she was ill—dying?' asked Joshua.

'It was her wish that you should not be troubled. "He will send for me or come for me when he wants me to go home again," she said. "He has higher things than me to think about." She was so earnest in this wish that we did not like to overrule her.'

'And nobody thought that she was dangerously ill,' explained Deborah. 'The doctor couldn't make her out. That was what he always said. It was one of the strangest cases he'd ever had to deal with. Some days she seemed so well and bright; and she was always industrious, anxious to be doing something for us; household work or needlework, it was all the same—we couldn't give her enough to do.'

'The journey here hurt her a great deal, I think,' said Priscilla, 'though she would never own to it. She walked a good bit of the way, I believe, and she was footsore and very weak when she came. I opened the door to her at dusk one evening, and I almost thought she was a ghost. "I want to be your servant, dear Miss Priscilla," she said, "as I was in the old happy days." "Why, Mrs. Haggard," said I, "what would your honoured husband think of such a notion?" But I'd hardly got out the words before she fell down in a faint at my feet; and for a week after that we had her laid up, and as low as could be.'

'And you never wrote to me about her!' cried Joshua, with agonised reproach.

'Well, the truth was we didn't like. We thought there was something wrong—a family quarrel perhaps, second marriages often turn out so—and the poor thing seemed to have come to us for refuge, and clung to us so; and if ever we talked of writing to you she seemed so distressed. And we had always been fond of her, and had missed her dreadfully after her marriage. She seemed like a daughter to us now she had come back; and I'm sure we nursed her and took care of her in her illness as if she'd really been a daughter, as I know Mr. Martin will bear witness.'

'You did,' said the minister; 'she could not have had better nursing or kinder treatment.'

'It was only just at the last that there was any mention of danger,' continued Deborah. 'On Saturday morning the doctor found her very low, poor dear, and her mind was wandering a little. He seemed quite distressed as he came down-stairs with me, as if it was a shock to him to find her so. "I don't at all like her looks this morning, Miss Webling," he said; "I begin to be afraid we shall lose her." I never had such a turn in my life. Poor Priscilla and I were almost beside ourselves with grief, and it was as much as I could do to write you a letter, begging you to come at once. You don't seem to have received that letter.'

'No, it must have been delivered after I left home. The post is so slow; you should have sent a messenger. Tell me, for God's sake—did she die happy, and did she love me at the last?'

'At the last, and always,' answered Mr. Martin earnestly. 'She bared her heart to me. I knew all its secrets, its waverings from the right, its weakness. She had always loved and revered you. She had been tempted, poor child, and her fancy had strayed to another for a little while—only a little while. Heart and mind were true to her duty. She was worthy of your fondest love; she was worthy of your deepest regret.'

'And I cast her from me, I repudiated her, I spurned her as the vilest of sinners! O friend, can her injured spirit look down upon me from heaven, and pity? Can God ever pardon my sin? He gave me this sweet flower to wear in my bosom, and I cast it from me, and trampled it under foot. I have steeped my soul in sin, I have dyed my hands with blood!'

The two spinsters and the minister looked at each other with an awful significance. These remorseful utterances seemed to them the tokens of a wandering mind. That this man, their model and pattern of uprightness, could deeply err came hardly within the limits of belief.

CHAPTER XVII.

'BETWEEN TWO WORLDS.'

THE days wore on very slowly for Naomi in her father's absence. Her heart was weighed down with anxiety on his account; but he had told her not to follow him, and, anxious though she was, she obeyed implicitly. A great burden had been taken from her mind by Joshua's confession. Bitter as it was to know that her lover had fallen by her father's hand, that the bright young life had been snapped short off, like a blossom from its stalk, in a burst of sinful passion, yet there was all the difference in the world between a fair fight and a dastardly assassination; and she was able now to think of her father as of other duellists she had heard and read about, red-handed sinners all, but not beyond the reach of human pity.

She was reconciled even to the idea of her father's prolonged absence, of a separation which might extend over years. It would be better, happier for him to go out into untrodden fields, and do difficult work, for his Master's sake. This pious labour would be his penance: in heathen lands he would find cities of atonement, from whose gates he might come forth loosed from the burden and stigma of his crime. She had longed herself to go into strange lands and teach heathen children the Gospel. What more natural than that her father, with his consciousness of a terrible sin to be expiated, should desire to brave dangers and endure hardships and trials in the great cause?

'Let him come back to me ten years hence, old and bent and gray,' said Naomi, 'and I will praise God for His bounteous mercies. I will say that our lives have been full of blessings even after all our sorrows.'

This was her prayer—that he might go forth as a messenger of the Gospel, and do his work of expiation, and come back to her purified and happy. It was the old heroic Greek idea of atonement, only in a Christian and better form.

A letter had come from Penmoyle for Joshua,

and was laid aside, unopened, awaiting tidings from him. No one supposed that the letter was of any particular importance. What they all waited for anxiously was a letter from Joshua himself.

It was Thursday, and Oswald Pentreath had been lying in the family vault for many days and nights. It seemed a natural thing already to think of him resting there with his ancestors, and it was almost possible to forget that he had lain for nearly a year in the darkness of the deserted mine, none knowing his fate. Strange how soon poor human nature resigns itself to the inevitable. Arnold bore the annihilation of all his hopes about his brother better than he could have supposed it possible to bear so heavy a blow. That agonising grief which he had felt when he supposed Oswald the victim of a treacherous assassin was lessened by Joshua's confession. At least he had fallen face to face with death. The murderer had not crept behind him with uplifted knife, coming upon his victim in a ghostly silence. It had been a hard fate and a cruel one, but not so bad as this. And poor Naomi, the innocent sufferer from her lover's inconstancy and her father's sin—could he ever be sorry enough for her? could he ever be sufficiently kind, or gentle, or thoughtful for her dear sake? Consideration for her pleaded eloquently against his desire for revenge. Joshua must go unscathed, so far as human vengeance went, and take his punishment from God. This was the result of many a weary hour of thought that followed upon Arnold's interview with Naomi.

Thursday morning brought another letter from Penmoyle, in the same handwriting as the last, but directed to Judith instead of to Joshua.

Miss Haggard broke the seal with a slight tremor, while Naomi waited full of anxiety. Why had her father not written?

'Chestnut Cottage, Penmoyle,
Cornwall, June 26th.

'Dear Miss Haggard,—I hope you will pardon the above familiarity, but although we have not had the pleasure of meeting, you can be no stranger to one who loves and reveres your brother as I do.

'I deeply regret to inform you that Mr. Haggard now lies in a sadly precarious state. Indeed our doctor and another gentleman, summoned at his advice from Penzance, entertain little hope of his recovery. The shock caused by his wife's death, which took place prior to his arrival, caused an apoplectic stroke. He recovered consciousness after several hours, but has never been quite right in his mind since the seizure.

'Feeling assured that you and the rest of his family would desire to be with him at such a time, I hasten to communicate the sad state of affairs, and beg you to make whatever use you please of our small abode. It is entirely at your disposal, and my elder sister and self will consider it a privilege to do all in our power to ameliorate your sorrow by such attentions as sympathetic hearts can offer. Our poor Cynthia's funeral takes place to-day. It is perhaps a blessing that in your suffering brother's state of mind he is scarcely conscious of passing events.

'Awaiting your speedy arrival, I remain, dear Miss Haggard, your obedient servant,

'PRISCILLA WEBLING.'

Before she had read half this letter, Judith Haggard gave a shriek of horrified surprise, and her niece looked over her shoulder and read it with her. The two women stood side by side, devouring the lines with white agonised faces, each in her own way feeling that this sorrow was the deathblow to all hope. James was in the shop, busy, happy, ignorant of this evil. He was whistling the last popular melody as he went about his work. How awful it seemed to hear him!

Naomi's grief found no outlet in tears or sobs or passionate speech. She stood with the letter in her hand, her lips trembling.

'The coach, aunt, the coach!' she gasped. 'Is it too late?'

'Gone half an hour, child; we must have a post-shay. Jim!'

The shrill voice rang through house and shop, and Jim appeared with a scared face at the parlour-door.

'What's the matter, aunt?'

'Your father's dying, and we're going to him. Get us a post-shay.'

Jim looked from one to the other in awful wonder. Naomi tried to speak, and, failing, gave him Priscilla's letter.

'What!' he cried, hurriedly reading, 'the poor little stepmother dead and buried! Has the world come to an end?'

'You unfeeling boy!' exclaimed Judith. 'To think of anybody else when your father's in such a state!'

'Father will come round again, please God; but poor little Cynthia—buried yesterday—so young and pretty! Isn't it dreadful?'

'Go for a chaise, Jim, for pity's sake,' cried Naomi. 'Father may die while you stand wondering there. O, let me go to him, let me go! let me keep him back from death!'

James ran across to the First and Last, the only place in Combhaven where post-horses were to be had. There was a burst of sympathy from the stout landlord when he heard Jim's news. The chaise should be ready in ten minutes—the best horses in his stable.

It was half an hour before the chaise was at the door, despite the landlord's promises. Naomi and her aunt had put on their bonnets and packed a few necessaries in a carpet-bag, and had been waiting in the parlour ever so long, as it seemed to them, before an ancient yellow-bodied chariot, like that which had brought Joshua's young bride to Combhaven, pulled up before the garden-gate.

'You'll stay at home and mind the business till I can come back, Jim,' said Judith.

'I'd rather go to poor father; but perhaps it's best so,' answered Jim. 'But if he should be very bad, if there's no chance of his getting over it, you'll send for me, aunt. I should like to see him before—'

A sob strangled the young man's speech, and he went back to the house, leaving them to get into the carriage unassisted. Some one was at Naomi's side before she could mount the steps. It was Captain Pentreath, breathless with running.

'Naomi, I have just heard of your sorrow,' he said gently. 'One of our men told me as I came across the meadow. Dear sister, let me go with you. Let me go with you, Miss Haggard,' he added pleadingly to Judith. 'I should like to go—

to be of service to you, if I can—to ask your brother's pardon for my violence the other night.'

'You'd need be sorry for that, I think,' answered Judith. 'What's the good of your coming? He'll want to see his blood-relations, poor dear—that's natural; but it can't give him much pleasure to see you.'

'I may be of use to you on the journey. Let me come, Miss Haggard. Two unprotected women, anxious, agitated as you are, ought not to undertake such a journey. These post-boys are such ruffians. I shall be able to prevent loss of time, to insure you civil treatment.'

Judith relented a little. Post-boys were an exacting and difficult race—greedy of gain, capable of abandoning their helpless fare upon a lonesome highway, or of colleaguing with highwaymen for a defenceless traveller's spoliation. Perhaps Judith, though strong-minded enough at home, where every one trembled at her voice, felt that she should be a weak vessel abroad. She had never travelled farther than Barnstaple in her life; and to go up alone into the wilds of bleak and barren Cornwall—the very stronghold of witchcraft—a place where half the people were savage miners, and the other half wreckers and smugglers; and to be benighted, perhaps, on a moor where the Druids sacrificed human beings before the days of King Arthur!

These terrors were too much for Judith. The proffered escort of a courageous young man, open-handed and ready to make use of his purse for the gratification of post-boys, was not to be despised. He had brought a false charge against Joshua in an hour of temporary madness; but he had repented, and this act of to-day was a confession of his past folly. All Combhaven would know of it, and see how baseless he now felt his idea of Joshua's guilt to have been. Judith gave way, but maintained her dignity even in the moment of concession.

'It matters very little to me whether you come or stay,' she said. 'My mind's too full of my poor brother to care about anything else. But Naomi may be glad of your company on the dark roads—girls are so timid.'

'Indeed, aunt, I am not frightened,' exclaimed Naomi.

'I am coming with you,' said Arnold decisively.

There was a seat at the back of the vehicle, a kind of rumble, and into this he mounted, after despatching a small boy to the Grange with a message for Nicholas the butler, who was to send his master's valise on to Truro by the evening coach. Arnold would not ask so much as five minutes' delay, lest Judith should change her mind and decline his company. So the post-boy smacked his whip, and the chaise went rattling through the long village street, to the delight of the inhabitants, who flocked out of their dwellings to witness the unwonted spectacle.

A long journey at any time; a weary one for aching hearts. Naomi looked out of the carriage-window with dull eyes that roamed over hill and valley, wood and winding stream, and saw no comfort anywhere. Was the journey never to be over? she wondered, as the slow hours rolled on; was there never to be an end of those green hedgerows, and tangled honeysuckles, and clambering dog-roses, and dusty wayside ferns, and sudden hollows, and jutting walls of hill?—these perpetual hills, at the foot of which the travellers descended, to walk in mournful silence to the top, where all the glory of the valley below could not move Naomi's cold lips to a smile of gladness.

Arnold made no attempt at consolation. He entreated his companions to hope for the best, and after that made no further allusion to their grief. He talked to them very little, only showing himself anxious for their comfort and repose. He saved them all trouble about post-boys, or any of the details of their journey. They had nothing to do but be patient, and wait till darkness came, and the end. Even to eyes accustomed to the rustic seclusion of Combhaven, Penmoyle looked a curious out-of-the-world place as the post-chaise drove into the wide village street after sunset on that June evening. Lights twinkled feebly in two or three casements, wide apart and rare, as if the majority had gone to roost at curfew. There was one light much brighter than the rest, which seemed to Naomi to shine like a star. Some instinct of her heart told her that it was the candle in her father's sick-room.

'There,' she cried, putting her head out of

the window, and calling to the post-boy; 'stop there.'

But Arnold had made his inquiries at the beginning of the village, and the boy was already pulling up his horses. That lighted casement belonged to Chestnut Cottage. The approach of the carriage had been heard within, and Deborah's stiff curls were waving at the door, as she came out to receive her guests.

'O dear Miss Haggard; O dear Miss Naomi,' she gasped; 'thank God you are come!'

'Not too late!' cried Naomi, going into the house; 'not too late!'

'No, dear young lady, praised be Heaven! He has asked for you so often.'

'Take me to him, please—at once.'

'But you ought to be prepared for the change—'

'God will give me strength when his dear head is on my breast. Father, I am coming,' she cried, as if her voice would carry strength and new life to the sick man.

She went up-stairs as quickly as if she had known the corkscrew staircase all her life. The door of her father's room was open; the window opened wide to the summer night. The old-fashioned tent bedstead, with its dimity festooning and netted fringe, faced the door.

Who was it lying there, still as a stone figure, with a white strange face, and dark cavernous eyes—a face Naomi had never seen before? For a moment her heart failed, and she shrank away a step or two, as from something more awful than death. Was this her father?

Yes, the hollow eyes lighted up at sight of her, the livid lips moved tremulously, and then murmured, 'Naomi!'

In the next instant she was on her knees beside his bed, clasping the heavy hands, crying over him, kissing him with those passionate despairing kisses life gives to death.

'Dearest, I have come to nurse you, to bring you back to life. God will help me. I have been praying for you all through our long journey. Father, you will get well for my sake.'

'I am dying, Naomi. The doctor and my old friend Martin have both told me so. Do not cry, dear; I am suffering so little. The passage is made very easy for me. And I have an infinite inextinguishable faith in my Redeemer's love. I go to Him without fear. He has loosed me from the burden of my sin. Yes, Naomi, it is no idle boast. I feel and know that I am forgiven. My punishment has been awarded here. My broken heart has reconciled me with my God.'

'You shall not die!' said Naomi. 'God cannot be so cruel as to part us now, when there is no cloud between us any more, when I can love you and honour you as I did in my childhood. Father, you will live for my sake.'

'No, dear, I have done with earthly life. God sent His stroke in mercy when I came into this house and found my darling dead. O Naomi, my latter days have been full of sin. I have been the slave of passion. And yet I might have been so happy. I can see her still—sitting in the sunshine—hair like spun gold—so helpless and lovely, so ignorant of good and evil—like Eve when God gave her to Adam.'

His mind wandered a little after this. All through the night he lay in the same attitude, a corpse-like figure, a soul hovering between life and death. Naomi never stirred from her seat beside his pillow, save to kneel and pray. Judith and Priscilla sat a little way aloof, watching the two, only coming nearer at intervals to moisten the sick man's lips with a feather dipped in brandy.

About an hour after daybreak Arnold, who had spent the night in the parlour below, came slowly up the stair, and stood on the threshold. Joshua had been lying for a long time with his eyes closed, breathing heavily, and his watchers had supposed him sleeping; but at the sound of Arnold's cautious footfall he opened his eyes, and those restless hands of his fastened with a nervous grasp upon the coverlet.

'Is that Captain Pentreath?' he asked his daughter.

'Yes, dear father.'

'Let the others go away,' looking dimly round at the two women; 'I want to be alone with you and him.'

Priscilla and Judith left the room, full of wonder.

'You got my letter?' he said.

'Yes, Mr. Haggard; and I am here to ask your forgiveness for the accusation I brought against you. When I found my poor brother in his secret grave I believed him the victim of a murderer. I am willing now to believe that he was the victim of his own folly, and that he willingly staked his life against yours.'

Joshua was silent. Some kind of struggle—whether bodily or mental those who watched him could not tell—was racking him. His nether lip worked convulsively; the veins stood up darkly purple from the broad strong brow.

'My letter told the truth,' he said after that painful pause, 'but not all the truth. I am going to face an offended God—going to Him confident in His illimitable mercy. Naomi, do not hate me when I am dead;' his hands wandered helplessly for a little, and then he clasped them round her neck, and let his head fall on her shoulder; 'do not hate me, dear. Your lover was murdered. He was generous, and I was a dastard. We stood up, face to face, each with a pistol in his hand. I was to count three, he told me, and then take aim. But as I lifted my hand to aim at his heart I saw his arm flung up, his pistol pointed to the sky. It was but an instant, fleeter than a breath, before I fired straight at his breast. It was thirty years since I had pulled a trigger —not since I was an idle lad, and went rabbit-shooting with my father's old blunderbuss. Yet my aim was deadly. The bullet pierced his heart. He had fired in the air. I had just time enough to see and understand what he was doing before I killed him. This was the crime that weighed upon my soul and dragged me down to the pit. O God, I can see him now, with his face lifted up, the sun shining on it, his arm raised to fire in the air. It was but a flash, scarce time for thought, but when it was over I knew myself a murderer. O God, only an instant between everlasting glory and eternal condemnation, unless Thine infinite sacrifice can blot out mine iniquity.'

There was silence. Naomi's face was buried in the coverlet. Arnold walked across to the open window, and stood there looking out at the gray morning sky, deeply thoughtful.

'My God, my sin is heavy,' ejaculated Joshua

after an interval; 'Thou only knowest my temptation. I, who had preached against duelling, became a duellist; I, who had taught men brotherly love, stained my hands with my brother's blood. Only in illimitable mercy can I find hope; and who shall tell the sinner his case is hopeless when God has given the promise of forgiveness?'

He lay for a long time after this in a state that was almost unconsciousness. The doctor came and felt his pulse, and told them that he was slowly sinking. It was only the vigour of his constitution which had held out so long against death. The nobly-built frame had wrestled involuntarily with man's last enemy, while the spirit yearned to pass the mystic river, and rest in the fair land beyond.

That day wore on, and the night which followed it, and another long summer day, which seemed to Naomi different even in the colour of its sky from every other day in her life. The sunshine climbed the whitewashed wall, and touched with brighter gold the tarnished gilding of the old oval picture-frames, and glorified the old cups and saucers and quaint little pottery jars on the narrow chimneypiece;

and still Joshua lay, awfully motionless, with his dull eyes turned to the light.

It was sunset when the dreaded change came. They were all on their knees praying silently when Joshua lifted himself up in the bed, and stretched out his arms towards that fading glory in the western sky.

'Cynthia—chosen—beloved,' he cried; 'innocent as a little child—ignorant of evil! Of such is the kingdom of heaven.'

And so, with a long-drawn shivering sigh, he fell back upon the pillow; and, as the sun went down behind a dark range of moorland, this little lamp of light went out with it, no less secure of resurrection.

EPILOGUE.

Joshua Haggard has been lying in his quiet grave among the Cornish hills just three years. It is midsummer time again, and the long straggling village of Combhaven is looking its gayest, beautified by Nature, and not by art. There is an unaccustomed life and stir in the place—people dressed in their best clothes, new bonnet-ribbons as rife as butterflies, every one upon the tiptoe of expectancy—and Naomi Haggard standing by the open parlour-window, very pale, in a gray Quaker-like silk—almost as pretty a gown as that wedding-dress she gave away four years ago; but it was not her father's hand this time which tested the quality of the silk, or her father's blessing which made the gift sweet.

Naomi has been an independent young woman for the last three years; for Joshua Haggard's will, made immediately after Oswald's dismissal, left his only daughter the five thousand pounds which had been intended as her marriage portion. She has suffered her aunt's domestic tyranny none the less meekly because of this independence. She has lived her quiet life in the old familiar home, so desolate without her father, and has taught her classes in the Sunday-school, and helped the new minister by many a quiet service, and held her place in the hearts of the Dissenters of Combhaven, who still honour Joshua's memory as that of a great and good man. This is Naomi's consolation. No shame or dishonour has ever been attached to her father's name in the public mind. The secret of Oswald's fate is known to none living save Arnold and herself.

To-day is a great day for Naomi—the happiest she has known since her father's death; for the memorial chapel—the new Bethel which she has built with a portion of her inheritance—is to be opened to-day. A fair lofty building of gray stone—a little too much like a corn-exchange on a small scale for the improved taste of this latter part of the century, but in those days a temple of exceeding beauty. There are four long straight windows on each side, an oak pulpit and reading-desk, a commodious gallery, and a Doric portico; and in the eyes of Combhaven the edifice is second only to Exeter Cathedral and Barnstaple Market.

To Naomi's mind the fairest thing in the brand-new chapel is a brazen tablet in front of the gallery bearing this brief inscription:

'This Chapel was erected in affectionate remembrance of Joshua Haggard, Minister.'

Naomi leaves the chapel after the opening service leaning on Arnold Pentreath's arm, tearful, but not altogether unhappy. Friends gather round her, and congratulate her, and are warm in their praises of the new Bethel; but it is to be noticed that there is an unwonted reverence in the tone of these old acquaintances, and that Mrs. Spradgers, notorious for extravagance in millinery, drops a low curtsy to Miss Haggard, instead of extending her pudgy hand in its black-lace glove.

Standing on the threshold of the new chapel,

Naomi stands also on the threshold of a new life. Her lover—faithful and unchanging through his three years' apprenticeship—is by her side, and to-morrow is to be their wedding-day.

THE END.

www.ingramcontent.com/pod-product-compliance
Lightning Source LLC
Chambersburg PA
CBHW031248250426
43672CB00029BA/1385